Tough-Minded Parenting

TOUGH-MINDED
Parenting

JOE BATTEN
WENDY HAVEMANN ▪ BILL PEARCE
GAIL PEDERSEN

BROADMAN PRESS
NASHVILLE, TENNESSEE

© Copyright 1991 • Broadman Press
4260-48
Dewey Decimal Classification: 649
Subject Heading: PARENTING//CHILD DEVELOPMENT
Library of Congress Catalog Card Number: 91-18216
Printed in the United States of America

Library of Congress Cataloging-in-Publication Data

Tough-minded parenting / Joe Batten . . . [et al.].
    p. cm.
  Includes bibliographical references.
  ISBN 0-8054-6048-9 : $14.95
  1. Parenting—United States. 2. Parenting—United States—Moral
and ethical aspects. 3. Values—Study and teaching—United States.
4. Child development—United States. I. Batten, Joe D.
HQ755.8.T67 1991
649′1—dc20   91-18216
                                                   CIP

To our children and grandchildren:
Erin, Jordan, Kyle, Michael,
Shawne, Steven, and Susan.
As a good tree is known by its fruit,
We are proud to be measured by these.

Contents

Foreword

A number of years ago I showed a Joe Batten management film to a group of teachers at a seminar I was presenting on positive attitudes. Later the feedback was fantastic. "Why many of the same techniques that make great managers could produce great teachers and great parents," a number of the teachers commented.

Tough-Minded Parenting, expecting the best from yourself and your children, is to me, a breakthrough. It is a book about the very future of America.

I've heard it said many times that the future of America is its children. Perhaps it would be more significant to say that the future of America will depend upon today's parents and the way they teach their children, the way they treat their children, and the way they love their children.

Perhaps my positive attitude is slipping, but I am deeply disturbed about the problems that we face in America today. Our education system is not working. Crime rates, especially among our children, are soaring. The drug problem has not lent itself to a solution. Just recently I visited a local school to speak for a room full of fourteen- and fifteen-year-old pregnant girls. Our newspapers are filled with tales of violence and destruction. I no longer feel safe walking the streets at night in many cities I visit.

If every American parent could and would read this book and begin to apply the powerful concepts and techniques that it contains, I believe we could resolve all of the problems I have just cited.

America today is a nation in deep need of a powerful set of family values. The sound foundation of the American family has disintegrated and the whole structure of our nation is in jeopardy.

This is a book by and for parents. It is a joint effort, a symposium of wisdom and experience both from today and from the past.

This is a book that can make a difference. It is a book about love and about vulnerability and understanding. It is a practical how-to book that avoids the psychological mumbo jumbo which has deluded so many permissive parents for the past few decades.

This is a book that asks tough questions. Better yet, it is a book that provides the answers that can make a difference in a child's future.

"Expect the best," is a phrase that I have heard from Joe Batten for many, many years. I've seen that phrase work miracles for managers. I've seen it turn whole departments and whole companies around. I know, deep in my heart, the power of that phrase and that concept: "Expect the best." And yet, many teachers and many parents in America have come to expect either the worst or mediocrity from our children. As a result children in America are testing far behind the children of other nations. Far too many children are not being challenged to discover that greatness that is within them.

I do not claim that this book is a cure-all. But I do believe that if the family will assume its God-given responsibility to our children then we will see a bright new future for the world.

ART FETTIG

Preface

At the very core of modern civilization—the motor of the world— is the family. All that is good, bad, or indifferent in every society, old and new, flows out of the health and effectiveness—or lack thereof—of the family.

Many segments of our society seem to be in pain. We are in a vicious cycle of self-reproach, self-denigration, and uncertainty. Negativism abounds, and finger-pointing seems to be the order of the day. We hear references to "our last days as a great nation," or to "a society under siege." We hear that "the family is out of date," and that "kids these days are going down the tubes."

What about it? Are we really? We feel there are serious problems. We also hold some strong, positive, hopeful views on our future possibilities.

But before examining these problems and possibilities, let's seek some perspective, an overview. The highly respected historian, Arnold Toynbee, says:

> Of the twenty-two civilizations that appear in history, nineteen of them collapsed when they reached the moral state that the United States is in now. The average age of the world's great civilizations has been 200 years. All nations have progressed through this sequence:
>
> From bondage to spiritual faith
> From spiritual faith to great courage
> From courage to liberty
> From liberty to abundance
> From abundance to selfishness

From selfishness to complacency
From complacency to apathy
From apathy to dependency
From dependency back again to bondage

Where do you think we are now? It is crucial for us to understand and believe that history does not have to repeat itself. New possibilities for greater human growth and actualization are all around us. For instance, network and cable television do not have to remain a vast spawning ground for violence, irresponsible sex, and all the permissive and expedient patterns of behavior which appear to be glorified currently to millions of American family viewers. It is our contention that all media can be very effectively used for stimulating human potential.

We present in this book a "tough-minded" solution.

The tough mind is resilient. It expends the energy to set and maintain reasonable boundaries while allowing room for growth—inside a framework of clear values. We believe deeply that a tough mind and a tender heart are one and that a transcendent faith—a living and growing belief in God—is crucial to tough-minded family living.

The hard mind is likely to hold to an extreme—being either rigidly intolerant of deviation or permissive of any behavior that one wishes to try. Neither extreme takes real effort or thought. Neither extreme works.

Often, the complex, sophisticated-appearing solutions are really the easy choices, while the simple solutions that we have known all along may be the tough but right choices. Often, if a solution seems complicated, it is assumed to be effective. The authors of this book believe that a simple but joyful set of values, examples, and expectations can make the difference in homes, schools, businesses, and other institutions.

True toughness is strong enough to be flexible, not hard and rigid. The tough mind opts for the joy of taking the strenuous, growing route. Such a mind is open, accepting, growing, resilient, and caring. Tough-minded people thrive on reaching, stretching, and confronting possibilities.

In this book, we recognize that the future of our families, our society, indeed of the world, will rise or fall in direct proportion to the presence, understanding, and practice of positive values. All human behavior, all striving, all significant success must reflect pervasive morality, or that endeavor, person, or undertaking *fails*.

It is our belief that the best way to think of child development is to see it as the growth of the child's value system. The child's values determine who that child becomes. Our values lead to our self-esteem. We respect and love ourselves because we have a way to measure our own worth.

Each family must create its own positive value system. We propose such values as these:

• The truth, when used warmly, wisely, and skillfully, liberates both children and adults to discover and reach their real potential.

• We find ourselves by losing ourselves in service to our children, other people, our country, and our personal faith.

• The more we give of healthy love, reasonable and stretching expectations, understanding and compassion, the more we will receive.

• We need to focus on our own and our childrens' existing and potential strengths, understanding that what we usually call a weakness is actually an absent, unused, or undeveloped strength.

• Giving and accepting consistent earned praise is a powerful reflection of integrity. Giving and taking credit lets us see our own value.

• Integrity and strength are the same.

For readers who have the will and desire to apply these values, we offer specific ways to use them. Throughout this book, we show how to apply your positive values to some of the real problems and real opportunities parents face in the real world. We cannot, of course, include every problem and opportunity that readers will encounter. We have tried to include the common ones that most parents will recognize and are most likely to face. We have tried to present them seriously but also, when possible, with the humor that we advocate as part of the healthy approach to family life.

These are ideal goals; they are hard to reach. We must say, in the honesty that we advocate for parents, that we, too, are still trying to reach them fully in our own lives and in our families. We who wrote this book are still striving to build families which:

- Develop family and personal missions based on faith.
- Focus on what a person can do, rather than how badly they have done or may do.
- Practice candor with each member of the family. (Candor means honesty applied with a helpful purpose and with concern for the other persons feelings.)
- Recognize that you gain confidence and courage every time you meet a family situation head on instead of deferring or pretending it isn't there.
- Recognize that the outcome of confronting problems is growth.
- Avoid developing scapegoats within the family or outside the family as excuses.
- Make sure that openness and vulnerability are rewarded and encouraged.
- Carefully and caringly develop behavioral limitations aimed at assuring safety and enhancing growth.
- Feel, express, and exemplify sincerity.
- Discover the joy and value of giving earned praise freely.
- Feel grateful to those who have helped you become what you are. Gratitude can become a state of mind and a way of life. Blaming others for what you are not is futile.
- Avoid putting others down, trying instead to compete only with yourself through thoughts and actions that build.
- Do your best, and accept that you can do your best and sometimes not succeed.
- Discover the renewing and empowering joy of compassion.

Our most precious gift is the capacity to make choices. Will you—

- Choose to be happy?
- Choose to build, renew, and enrich those you love?
- Choose to relish your uniqueness as a person and that of others?
- Choose to pursue the power of love?
- Choose to pursue the power of faith?
- Choose to empower and renew yourself and your family?

- Choose to build, not to destroy, in every word and action to your children and others?
- Ask for help when you need it?

Since we cannot live in neutral, we are always either building or destroying with every thought, word, or action.

It's your choice!

The Pledge of the Tough-minded Parent

On My Honor, As a Parent, I will do my best to:

Expect the best from myself and my children.

Share love, laughter, and life with my children.

Develop and be guided by the highest faith, vision, and values.

Be truthful and honest with my children at all times.

Teach and lead by my example.

Encourage my children to share fully in our lives together.

Accept my children enthusiastically and vulnerably.

Find and develop the strengths in every family member.

Change yelling, telling, and commanding to asking, listening, and hearing.

Demonstrate a clear link between expectations, performance, and outcomes.

1

Our Panel of Experts

Parents today are more afraid more often. Parents fear they will be overwhelmed by what looks to be more and more an impossible task—raising children to become decent and happy human beings. This is our most important job. We have one chance with each child. We'd better develop the ability, the knowledge, and, most importantly, the confidence to do it right.

Human beings are marvelously creative. Our most wonderfully creative act is the creating of new human beings. A person is not merely born. Indeed, birth is just the beginning. A full-blown, individual person is truly created by human experience out of the potential that is present at birth. Each infant is a wonderful and unique bundle of potential waiting to be formed into a person through experience.

Who a person becomes is mostly a creation in and by families. While it is true that each person has many significant growing experiences outside of the family, it is also clear that the most important experiences are those provided in the family, by parents.

Parenting is our most important single activity.

Human beings are producers. People everywhere in the world are engaged in making a great variety of things. We produce clothing, shelter, food, works of art, ideologies, medicines, weapons, new information—everything from soup to nuts and from ships to symphonies. Productivity, creativity, making things we need or want—these are the visible activities which make us human.

In our families, we create children who will be creators in their turn. Parenting is our most important single human activity, and children are

17

our most important product. We are increasingly challenged as we try to prepare our children for a rapidly changing world.

How well are we doing in this vital area? Do we believe we can do the job? Do we have confidence in our ability to be parents? Are we in danger of giving up on this most important human activity?

People today have given up in many other areas of their lives. We are becoming more and more prone to turn to the experts for the handling of every problem. Whenever we feel the slightest anxiety or fear, whenever we have a dispute, or whenever we are faced with a difficult decision, we call on the experts to tell us what to do. This seems to be especially true in raising children. We seem to run for help to the experts whenever a problem arises.

We got into this habit honestly enough. There are, indeed, many truly helpful experts out there, professionals who can see you through a problem when you truly cannot handle it by yourself. When you really need the experts, select them carefully and use them.

Parents, however, have been raising children longer than there have

---

Seeking Help

We advocate self-reliance and independence. At the same time, we advocate realizing your own limitations, and seeking help when you need it.

How can you know when you need help as a parent?

How can you know just what help you need?

The telephone books are filled with listings; almost too many to know where to begin. Here are some hints that may help you:

• Start with someone you know and have confidence in already. Your clergyman may be a good place to start. Your child's schoolteacher or school counselor is also a good resource. They will know, or can direct you to someone who does know, what services are available.

• Talk about the concerns with your family. Share the problem.

• Approach the counselor with the belief that you can learn how to deal with the problem. View the problem as solvable.

• Have faith that you will be strengthened to solve it.

• Don't accept permanent dependency on an expert as an answer.

been parenting experts. How did our great-grandparents function without them? Somehow, for many centuries, most families managed the problems faced in raising children fairly well. How did they do it? Can we do it today?

In the past few decades we have learned many valuable things that have truly improved the lives of children. We know a lot about nutrition and how it affects children's growth. We know much more about how children develop physically, mentally, and emotionally.

We are no longer hiding and denying any unpleasant facts about family life. We are much more alert to the existence of previously undetected incest and physical abuse than we used to be. We know more about the effects of verbal and emotional abuse. There is much less chance of exploitation of child labor for profit than there was in the past. We are much more aware of the importance of equal opportunity for boys and girls, men and women. We owe much to the many fine advocates for children who have contributed to these and other improvements.

Evil and ignorance are not new in the families of the world, any more than are goodness and wisdom. What is new is parental dependence— handing parental decision-making responsibility to someone else.

This dependency goes far beyond parenting. We turn to the experts to resolve our personal and interpersonal problems because we do not have confidence in our ability to solve them for ourselves. When we over-depend on the experts, we avoid developing our own strengths and capabilities.

What lies at the root of our growing dependence? We are constantly bombarded with warnings of how every move we make with our children may scar them for life. We are losing our confidence. We are terrified of making mistakes. We are failing to develop the ability and the will to face other people and discuss disputes or issues. We are failing to ask, listen, and hear. We have become dependent on professionals to do our thinking for us.

This dependence costs us dearly in every way. There has arisen a whole generation that knows primarily a legalistic, adversarial approach to solving interpersonal problems. The legal process has become so enmeshed in our lives that we are becoming afraid to communicate honestly. We fear we may accidentally place ourselves in legal jeopardy. We fear we may cause an ᵔmotional problem. We are becoming fearful of offering help to others, even members of our families, lest we create some kind of mental health problem. We fear that we may even be sued for our trouble. We are increasingly governed by the fear of error. Only turning to an expert is "safe."

The Panic-Button Parent

Fear of self-reliance, underdevelopment of judgment, and a sense of inadequacy work together with an unfortunate trend in our society: the pressure to produce the "right kind" of child. Worse yet, we let others decide for us what the "right kind" of child is!

Many parents tend to think: "Our child must be the first to walk, the first to talk, the most skilled at grasping objects or ideas, the first at any developmental measure. Our child must somehow be highly creative and independent and perfectly behaved."

These parents aspire to the super-clean, super-right image of the modern child. Children and parents are in a social fishbowl in which their every action, every event, every clothing item, and especially anything definable as a developmental blunder, is perceived to be under critical scrutiny.

The child who appears to fall short of perfection causes real anxiety in these parents. Such parents seem to want their child to make up for the parent's own regrets in life. Such parents seem to want to re-live their life through the life of the child without making the same mistakes! This is often a reflection of the parent's own feelings of inadequacy, their own need for approval and praise.

Parents often live in dread of failure. This is partly because, as parents, we are constantly reminded of the ways in which children can "go wrong." Every day we read and hear stories of youth involved in all of the perils of childhood and adolescence. As parents, our greatest nightmares are that some of these bad things will happen to our children and that we will be to blame.

Our fear often is that every hint of failure, every deviation from perfection means that something is "terribly wrong with our child." With fingers poised over the panic button, we expect—and therefore we often find—failure as parents. We then frantically seek out the experts who can tell us how we should raise our children. If problems still arise after seeking expert advice parents can then pretend it's not their fault.

"And Then We Ran"

Recently, one of the authors made an audio tape of some of the childhood happenings in "the old neighborhood" of a central city area in the 1940's. This tape was made at the request of his children, who had heard these stories a lot. Noting that the stories often ended with the phrase, "and then we ran," the children labelled them "Then We Ran" stories.

These stories ranged from tales of hanging strings of cans onto the bumpers of cars at stoplights, to messing up wet concrete, to tossing eggs into traffic, to shooting b-b's at a reportedly "crazy" man who lived in a local salvage yard down by the river.

We were frequently caught. Our parents did not seek "expert advice" on those occasions. We children were not assumed to be "maladjusted" because of our actions. Our parents seemed to have no doubts as to what to do. They were confident in their strengths, and so were we!

Before the Panic Button Was Invented

What was a parent's world like when our grandparents, and their grandparents, were children? Were children being successfully raised before the experts came along? How can we judge the quality of child rearing in the past? Perhaps by looking at the product, at the kinds of adults that those children turned out to be, at the wonders they have achieved.

Remarkable advances in the human condition clearly have occurred in the last few generations as the result of the creativity, the industry, and the strong character of those recent generations. We are surrounded by evidence of their abilities, and we owe our way of life to their courage in the face of hardships.

Not all the children of those generations, of course, were well raised. At the same time as these great advances were going on there was also some real human misery. Many people of that time came from inept and even cruel family situations. As a result, many of them had serious

problems. We live with some of the ill results today. These are traditions that we still must work to overcome.

Still, the achievements of recent generations reflect the work of some
outstanding human beings. Consider the obstacles they successfully
overcame. There must have been some good parenting going on to
produce such people. Where did these courageous, talented, and productive people come from?

People are created in families.

How did those parents know what to do? Where did they get their
expertise? Not having "experts" to turn to, they handled this question
the same way in which they handled other problems they faced: they
turned to their own resources and the wisdom of their heritage. They
tapped the wisdom of their families and of others in their communities.
And it worked!

That same wisdom is our heritage today.

Of course, these parents did not know everything they needed to
know; no one does. But they knew where to turn for answers. They
turned to each other! They turned to the wisdom and common sense
that has been slowly developed over the countless centuries of human
family life—And they were not disappointed, because the answers to
parenting were there. They still are! The real "experts" are all around
us, and, indeed, within us.

For Family Discussion

Think of some of the strong, older people whom you know and admire.
Now try to picture their parents. Imagine asking those parents how they
would feel about consulting a parenting expert to help them make decisions about their children.

What would they be likely to say?

What does it men to say: "Only by struggling do we become stronger"?

Our Panel of Experts

Following our grandparents' example, let us now turn to each other.
Let us seek out our own "experts."

In researching this book, we contacted dozens of parents of all ages whose record of success, and the testimony of their children, seemed to qualify them as possessing the tough-minded qualities that make up a good parent. These parents served as part of our "panel of experts" for the writing of this book. The good news is there were so many great parents that we had trouble keeping the numbers within bounds! Their letter are printed later in this chapter. You'll find them eminently qualified.

There was also another group of parenting experts available to us. This second part of our panel is available to everyone; they speak to us all through the great works in which the highest values and the wisdom of our culture are preserved. They include names familiar to all, and some names that may be more obscure. Some may surprise you. Many of them speak to us from ancient history when only fathers and sons were the focal point of child raising. It is interesting to consider the era in which some of these words were written and see how they now apply as well to daughters and sons, mothers and fathers.

Do any of these quotations sound familiar to you?

1. "From the moment of his birth the customs into which [an individual] is born shape his experience and behavior. By the time he can talk, he is the little creature of his culture."—Ruth F. Benedict, *Patterns of Culture*, 1934.

2. "The hand that rocks the cradle is the hand that rules the world."—William Ross Wallace, *The Hand That Rules the World*, 1819-1881.

3. "Give a little love to a child, and you get a great deal back."—John Ruskin, *The Crown of Wild Olive*, 1866.

4. "Love is the chain whereby to bind a child to his parents."—Abraham Lincoln, *Conversation at the White House*, 1866.

5. "Virtue is harder to be got than knowledge in the world; and, if lost in a young man, is seldom recovered."—John Locke, *Some Thoughts Concerning Education*, 1693.

6. "He that will have his son have a respect for him and his orders, must have a great reverence for his son."—Ibid.

7. "This above all: to thine own self be true, And it must follow, as the night the day, Thou canst not then be false to any man."—Shakespeare, *Hamlet*, 1564-1616.

8. "Children learn to creep ere they can learn to go."—John Heywood, *Proverbs*, 1546.

9. "The root of the state is in the family. The root of the family is in the person of its head."—Mencius, *Works*, 372-289 B.C.

10. "Never has a man who has bent himself been able to make others straight."—Ibid.

11. "Fathers, provoke not your children to anger, lest they be discouraged" Colossians 3:21, King James Version.

12. "Or what man is there of you, whom if his son [asks for] bread, will he give him a stone?" Matthew 7:9, KJV.

13. "Train up a child in the way he should go, and when he is old, he will not depart from it." Proverbs 22:6, KJV.

14. "Instill the love of you into all the world, for a good character is what is remembered."—*The Teachings of Merikare*, 2135-2046 B.C.

15. "Truth is great and its effectiveness endures."—*The Maximns of Ptahhotpe*, 2350 B.C.

16. "Teach him what has been said in the past; then he will set a good example. . . . Speak to him, for there is none born wise."—Ibid.

Letters from the Firing Line

The good news is that there really is a lot of good parenting going on. We invited a number of parents to share their experiences. These are parents who seem to be doing things that work! Each parent was asked to write on a single page what they believe to be the essence of a good parent and to write on a second page a letter to their parents, saying anything they were inspired to say.

We have found these "letters from the firing line" to be stimulating, insightful, and valuable. These writers constitute our second "panel of experts." You are invited to read each letter thoughtfully and thoroughly. Then feel free to write you own letter to your parents and discuss it with a partner.

In Memory I Can Hear My Girls Laughing

I think of a good parent as one who includes the children in every aspect of family life, responsibilities as well as the love and the fun.

The smallest one can learn to pick up and put away their toys as well as play with them. Maybe a girl or boy will never have to cook a meal, but it never hurts to know how.

Communication is the heart of it all—not watching TV as a family, but forgetting TV. Sometimes today even a meal together is a rare event, whereas families always used to be together, sharing ideas and thoughts as well as food.

Our extended family relationships are suffering—closeness of aunts, uncles, cousins, grandparents—not intentionally, I'm sure. TV has become a wedge separating families.

In memory I can hear my girls laughing, talking, singing, even playing games as they washed dishes. Has even the electric dishwasher become a wedge? Baking cookies—decorating them for Easter, Christmas, or birthdays—was a family time.

Schools fill time with extracurricular activities too much. There are good programs on TV for children, but how about reading on Grandma's lap?

A Bird's-eye view

It was easier for me to write of parenting than to pretend I was a child writing to a parent. It made me see more of a teenager's thoughts, though. But I am eighty-three years old and maybe more tolerant.

I have four children, eleven grandchildren, and "almost" twenty great grandchildren, so I have a bird's-eye view.
Dear Parent:

I want to tell you I want and need your approval even if I didn't act like it. I also want to be popular with my peers. I know these two ideas are not always compatible, but I don't know what to do about it.

I want my family to love each other and let me know it. I need something stable to hold onto.

Please be less critical, not just of me but of all I've been taught to believe in—church, government, school, teachers, and people around us. Look for the best. That old song you used to sing, "Accentuate the positive, eliminate the negative," may have something to it.

The world today seems so big and so alarming, and here I am in the middle of it all. I do need help even if I seem to shrug it off.

Consistency: The Safe Harbor

Consistency has to be my definition of the essence of good parenting.

If a parent can consistently set reasonable limits and be willing to establish and enforce consequences, a child will have a framework and will understand what is expected of him.

If a parent can consistently remember to praise a child, not just for accomplishments but for efforts and his individual qualities, that young person will know he is valued.

If a parent can consistently respect a child's individuality instead of expecting him to be a reflection of the parent, the child can feel free to grow.

Finally, if a parent can consistently be approachable for support, whether it be in the capacity of adviser or just as a good listener, the child will feel he has a sort of safe harbor.

"I Was The Best Thing that Happened"

Dear Mom and Dad:

The greatest thing you gave me (besides your love) was the belief that I could accomplish anything. I grew up thinking I was the best thing that happened to you.

The second thing is the sense of humor we all share. I grew up with laughter.

Daddy, you taught me the importance of friends. You can never have too many friends, you said. But to have a friend, you have to be a friend.

You always trusted me. I always understood if I were out and were going to be late, it was OK as long as I called. I was never told to come home immediately, and for that reason I never abused that trust. (Stretched it once or twice, but never abused it.)

You taught me respect for others. You taught and showed me love. For this I am grateful.

To close, I miss you both, love you, and, most of all, thank you for letting me become me.

Firm—Fair—Friendly

I believe parenting is a learning process for all members of the house-hold, with parents being presented with more opportunities for learn-

*ing than children. No one upon first becoming a parent can possibly
know all he or she needs to know.*

*Therefore, I think it is important to accept that fact and be willing to
learn and grow, tuning in to the needs of others; being positive as much
as possible; making a conscious effort to use more "do's" than "don'ts".*

*Consistency is an important word in parenting, setting guidelines,
boundaries, and allowing children to feel a part of the plan—having
objectives as a team.*

*Another top priority, I think, is to teach, through actions and words,
the values and purpose of life with reverence and respect to God. As a
result of such consistent guidance, I think self-images grow as well,
which is a most crucial part of life.*

Some brief thoughts collected through the years:

Be a 3-F Parent: Firm, fair, friendly.

Teach children value by valuing them.

Success breeds more success.

Self-esteem—a most precious gift from parents.

*Of course, keeping a sense of humor along the way is an absolute
necessity to make it all work!*

I Don't Remember Any Depression

Dear Mom and Dad:

*I'm thankful for so much that I had growing up with you both as my
parents. Even though many material possessions were not ours, I don't
remember feeling deprived. There was never a lack of love and warmth.
I remember a feeling of being a part of the team—of having a purpose
in life and working toward goals.*

*We (all eight of us children) grew up during a time of great changes.
Just imagine driving the team to town (before we had a car) to witnessing
space shuttles, and more amazing changes for each generation that are
hard even to imagine! Anyway, I'm glad I was part of that era and I
love passing some experiences on to my grandchildren!*

*You taught us by your example. Many times words weren't necessary.
I remember you were highly respected in the community, Dad, and
how proud I felt when you were on the school board.*

*At the time, I'm sure we didn't appreciate how hard you both worked
to keep all of us fed and clothed. As we grew up, we knew the 30's had*

been terribly hard times. I don't remember any depression or complaints in our home. I do remember stories read to us, homemade fun, radio listening, piano playing. I remember the chores, too: picking vegetables and preparing them for canning, feeding the chickens, working in the fields. Everyone worked, so it was just the natural thing to do and we didn't question it. I'm sure there were plenty of times you had problems getting us to finish a job to your satisfaction. I can remember procrastinating!

Mom, you were with us a little longer, and I'm so glad we got to know each other as adults. Even thought we were friends as I grew up, it's different later on, isn't it? How I'd love to have our grandchildren know you and to have you hold our new little granddaughter.

I thank God for you both being wise, down-to-earth parents and for giving us the tools to learn about God, life, love, and wisdom.

I look forward to seeing you again.

A Basic Religion They Can Hang Onto

When your children are young, they need to go to Sunday School and get a basic religion they can hang onto. If they get too involved in activities later they will at least have a basic religion to remember. Get involved in Sunday School and make it fun so the kids want to come. Have prayer before meals, and when they have their own family they will, too.

Read to your kids when they are small and get them to take an interest or concern in something or someone instead of just themselves. Teach them to share and not be selfish.

Do something together as a family. Set up family traditions that kids will always remember.

It's very important to be able to communicate with kids as they are growing up. Sometimes you have to act like a kid yourself in order to communicate.

Wow! What a Privilege!

Communication has always been a high priority for us. We wanted to truly communicate with our children in the hope that as the years went by we could move from "training" our kids to having the close relation-

ships we now enjoy with them. We wanted to prepare them for adult decision making.

We spent a lot of time talking, advising, and listening. To be sure that we were having good communication, we often asked the kids to tell us in their own words what they thought we parents were trying to say. In turn, we tried to tell them what we thought they were trying to say. Many times we found ourselves searching together as a family for just the right words. It took patience. We had to allow time. We needed to let them know of our love for them when communication was difficult. Our aim was to lead them to think things through, look at the alternatives, put them into words, and then choose.

This has paid many dividends. Our kids have learned to look at the issues separately from their personal involvement. They have learned to communicate under some pressure. Hopefully, they can handle the events and people they will find in the outside world. We hope they've learned that when things go wrong is when you most need someone who really loves and cares.

Wow! What a privilege to help prepare young lives and to see them mature right before our eyes! Naturally, we're proud parents. We recommend to anyone who can, enjoy this privilege as we have.

Now What?

To be perfectly honest, my parenting philosophy has changed over the years, or as I prefer to believe, my philosophy has "matured."

In the beginning, I thought I was the cause and Brian was the effect. Brian took four-hour naps because I was a wonderful and knowing mother. Then child number two was born. Chris took maybe three naps in his whole babyhood. What happened to the perfect mom?

With Chris, I realized that each child has his own personality, his own strengths. Now what? I decided it was our duty to mold but also but also to let these little personalities "be." I took all the parenting classes that said, "Don't stifle the child; let him be himself!" (No matter how obnoxious this child becomes). This wasn't exactly how I was raised, but I was going to be a friend to my kids!

Then child number three was born and my philosophy began to "jell." Now what? I believe children are truly a gift from God, loaned to us. If we do our jobs, at some point these children will leave us to go on to successful and happy lives of their own.

The gift of the child is the enjoyable part; the loan of the child is the hard part.

The gift is the joy a child gives. I love to listen to children, watch them when they play, cry with them when they hurt. A child's play is often his job, and he can be very serious about it. Adults should really pay attention to a child's reasoning. It often makes more sense than our own involved ideas!

The hardest part of child raising is the loan, having to give the child back to the world, because this is where the child becomes independent. He may push you, stretch you, and try you. He may need guidance; resist it. The tough part is the discipline and the teaching of respect and responsibility. To be a parent isn't a popularity contest. In fact, you may come in last once in a while. But if a child learns respect, becomes responsible, and is loved, that child can be himself and give himself to others. He will become a happy and responsible adult.

Parenting is a tough job, but I wouldn't miss it for the world!

Rock Me One Last Time—To Eternal Optimism

Mom, I still vividly remember the day I fell asleep on the [school] bus and was so embarrassed when the bus driver had to carry me to the lane. You must have watched the whole scene because you sat waiting in a rocking chair with a blanket to rock me when I walked in the door. I was a "big girl," nearly eight years old, and simply couldn't let you rock me. But you were there and that was what counted. You have always been there for me. As an adult, a trip home to me meant long talks until the wee hours of the morning and long walks through the timber with me talking and you steadfastly listening, offering a constant stream of encouragement.

You were there for the excitement of our marriage, the trauma of my doctoral exams, the graduation of my mate, and the birth of Adam. You played a tremendous role of supporter; you were never "in the way." I've always felt that we were very much alike. I look forward to a wonderful fate of turning out twenty-five years from now like you are at this moment. Now I can relate to so many more feelings as a mother myself. I only hope I will understand my son with that same sensitive spirit which you gave to me. We are kindred spirits, Mom. I often wish I would have let you rock me that one last time.

Dad, you and I have always "had a thing" as Mom says. I would do anything to get out of dishes to help you in the field, wood-shop, pond, or even the hog house! I watched you skillfully handle cattle, tenderly hold baby pigs, excitedly plant seeds, and thankfully harvest the crop. As a thirty-five-year-old mom myself, I still look forward to riding the rounds with you in the combine when we come to visit. You always found time to pick wild plums and strawberries, pausing just long enough to spot a deer or two. Our mushroom picking adventures have been outstanding: I remember picking until the darkness forced us to feel the hillside, nearly stumbling over a great big owl; being scared nearly to death as we headed home.

My philosophy of life has been based on your eternal optimism, Dad. I never remember a time when you weren't excited about farming, even through some pretty tough droughts. Life has become so rich for me by "always having something to look forward to" as you taught me. You have kept young by taking on large and small adventures. I thought I knew and loved you as much as I could until I saw you tenderly and lovingly hold our newborn son. Words can no longer express my love and respect for you, Dad. You are the best Dad to me, dad-in-law to my mate, and "poppa" for our son I could have ever dreamed to find.

Good Parents Make Mistakes

Why couldn't every child have as wonderful a family as I had? We had such great times, even though we had little money. We did things that many of my more affluent friends never did—traveled, created entertainment as a family group, met people, entertained guests. We learned tolerance of others, good manners, the ability to adjust to many different life-styles. There was always an adventure.

The life of our family revolved around the church, but was not dominated by it. We weren't led blindly into a solemn religious roundup. We were shown we had choices, and we could freely choose without guilt.

Good parents have respect for each other, and it shows in the way they deal with their children. They show by example how to live re-

sponsible, confident, mature lives. They pass on to their children their personal set of values, ethics, and morals, including religious beliefs. They recognize the individuality of each young life and adjust the interaction accordingly. In adversity, good parents show their humanity and express fears, doubts, and sadness. Good parents make mistakes but admit them and learn from them.

I hope my children look back on their childhood with such good memories as I have of mine.

We have said earlier that the secrets to good parenting are readily available to us all. Our culture is filled with true experts, past and present. Their words are there for us to read and to hear.

What is amazing is that they are so familiar! As you read and listen to these clear and simple guidelines, did you want to say, "I already knew that"? You're right. The secrets to tough-minded parenting are all around us and within us. But somehow we have lost the confidence to use the knowledge we have.

Our heritage is indeed filled with help and sources of wisdom about helping young people grow. We have, for instance, inherited a tradition of highly effective character-building organizations. Organizations such as the Scouts, the American Pony club, and the many church-centered youth organizations provide high ethical standards and positive values. They also encourage children to develop self-reliance.

The Art of Being

One of the key ideas in tough-minded living is an emphasis on *being* rather than *doing*. We believe that what you *are* will determine what you *do*. If the emphasis in raising children is to help them to *be* the best that they can *be*, both they and their families will be pleased with what they *do*.

One of the most famous and effective of these character building organizations is scouting. Since the growth and success of scouting, many other fine organizations for boys and girls have been built upon the same general model. There will be some of these available to almost anyone who reads this book, almost anywhere in the world.

For Family Discussion
"A Scout Is"

The scout law is one of the most straight-forward and most-quoted statements as to what a "good person" is to be. All of you will recognize it instantly.
"A scout is:

trustworthy	obedient
loyal	cheerful
helpful	thrifty
friendly	brave
courteous	clean
kind	reverent"

Scouts don't go around in their uniforms all the time. How do you know a scout when you see one? Is there something special that they do? No! There is something special that they are! Notice that the scout law does not tell a scout one thing about what to do. It simply says "A scout is" and then describes the traits a scout is expected to reflect.

The American Pony Club is another example of an organization designed to help children become successful and responsible. Youth in the pony club organization are expected to be responsible for themselves and their horse without parental or adult supervision. Each child's expectations are based upon his age and level of competence. Safety, horsemanship, and cooperation are emphasized. Living up to their own potential, having a lot of fun, and getting things done are stressed to children rather than beating each other in competition. The children compete against themselves.

Scouts and Pony Club are examples of organizations expecting the best.

Church-centered organizations offer good adult leadership and role models for children, providing examples of adults who seek spiritual guidance in their personal lives and who live by high values. These organizations often provide opportunities for children and youth to earn their way to camp; to participate in programs of reaching out to the community; or to extend charity and encouragement to persons who are elderly, ill, or just unfortunate. These organizations give young people a chance to practice their faith with others of their own age and to form the kinds of peer relationships that support what is being said and done at home.

Is it an accident that the roster of our top leaders is heavily represented by people who, as youngsters, were members of one of our nation's character-building organizations? As adults, they continued to be guided by values such as those developed at their church, learned in a special activity club, or set out in the scout law.

We encourage the involvement of your children in one of the many fine character-building organizations for young people. These organizations usually emphasize what a good person *is* rather than what a good person *does*: *be*ing rather than *do*ing.

You Can Be a Tough-Minded Parent

Tough-minded parenting is to be found in the wisdom we already have. We stand upon a foundation of experts stretching back literally thousands of years. We are surrounded by experts. We *all are* experts, if we will allow ourselves to believe it. You are, too!

You can confidently say: We have met the experts, and they are us.

2

Parenting Today: Does It Work?

Tough-minded parenting is a journey. It is a look at the parents and the children of the present and the past—a search for their wisdom and insight. We have researched across the nation, across the world, and throughout history for the best that is known as a guide for the parents of today.

The family exerts the most powerful influence in the world. This is true today; it has always been and always will be true. It is also the area of greatest need. In the family lies the secret to the future: the future of our own country, our way of life, and of the world. All will rise or fall with the family.

This idea may seem simplistic at first glance. We place it, however, in the context of alarms being raised about drug and alcohol problems, teachers dealing with disruptive and underperforming students, the health of the nuclear family, and even aging parents. The family is being subjected to pressures, disruptive influences, divisive forces, and degeneracy to an extent never before experienced.

Parents are feeling pushed and threatened by forces over which they believe they have no control—forces pulling the family structure apart at the seams. Our society seems in danger of "atomizing" into isolated, disconnected, self-centered individuals. The once integrated family is steadily disintegrating into nothing more than a houseful of separate persons who think mainly of themselves. Many fathers and mothers today simply want to get the children "raised" so that they can "relax and be secure." Many children today see the family as merely a source of food, shelter, and clothing from which they want to flee as soon as they can.

35

There are, of course, many healthy, happy families. In almost every instance, the truly happy family is one where the parents take a strong interest in the children; where all ideas are exchanged openly and freely. This is the family where parents have reached a point of inner peace and tough-mindedness.

The greatest contribution to the success of a family is the feeling on the part of family members that they are wanted, important, significant, and worthy of dignity. All too often a family values its members only in terms of what they *do* rather than for who they *are*. A child who feels unwanted, unimportant, insignificant, and without dignity may begin to seek for those things through antisocial behavior, experimenting with alcohol or other drugs, feigning illness, or even developing a genuine illness. The same is true of adults. Husbands, wives, fathers, and mothers need to feel significant, loved, and necessary for more than just producing the paychecks, doing the chores, or chauffeuring children.

Yes, the family is in trouble. Parents are reacting with fear when constantly confronted with new revelations of the prevalence of drugs, the spread of AIDS, the headlines stating that our children are falling behind the world in education. We're running scared! What can we do?

A strong, value-led family is based on love, high expectations and healthy spiritual faith. Building stronger, value-led families, is the only answer to the trouble we face. All of our other efforts are proving to be futile.

Before we discuss new tough-minded answers to these fears and dilemmas, we need to take a thorough look at the problem: where we are today, what's been tried, and why much of it hasn't worked.

Excerpts From the Media

Reports from the media bear out what is becoming increasingly clear to school professionals, youth authorities, and parents all across the country: *Too many of our children are in danger of being totally lost to their family, their communities, and TO THEMSELVES*.

Such efforts as media campaigns, anti-drug and safe-sex slogans and programs, or getting "back to basics" in education are at best having minimal impact. Certainly, while these efforts are not quite totally futile, the facts show that they are not coming close to providing the answers we need.

A great deal of effort certainly has been applied to help the youth of this country. Through schools we have set up well-thought-out-programs, brought in speakers, created new curricula, trained teachers and counselors, and spent huge amounts of money trying to direct the attitudes and actions of our children into more positive and healthy directions. The results, however, are not encouraging. Consider the following excerpts from media reports of the last two years:

1. On November 10, 1989, the *Wall Street Journal* reported on the results of an exemplary antidrug program at Bainbridge High School in a peaceful, affluent community near Seattle. The program failed. Despite twelve years of exposure to "one of the most intensive and innovative anti-drug education programs in the country," a recent study showed that "as many as 70 percent of students use drugs or alcohol weekly" and "approximately 5 percent of students in junior high and high school are chemically dependent."

Evaluations of the program show that the goal of providing information has been attained. The article states, "Students in the program became unusually well informed about drugs and school." And, they "agreed such substances are bad for them." Still, they were quoted as calling the antidrug exercises "a joke," and many of those students who are the best achievers admit to getting drunk often at parties.

The report goes on to say that the California Department of Education has spent over 45 million dollars during the past three years on drug-education programs in the schools. These programs emphasize decision-making skills, assertiveness training, and self-esteem building, as well as facts and information on drugs and alcohol—in short, all

---

A Glimpse of Truth at Bainbridge

The Bainbridge School Superintendent stated in the article that parents must "abandon the notion of parenting in absentia." He seems to understand that the family is the true key to the problem—and to the solution.

of the qualities believed to be needed by young people if they are to avoid using drugs.

Bainbridge authorities reacted to the news of the failure of these efforts by deciding to try more of the same! The same program will be continued "with innovations" and with "greater emphasis on social skills and assertiveness."

2. *The National Parents' Resource Institute for Drug Education* reported in September 1989, that while junior high use of beer has declined from about 40 percent to about 36 percent in the five years between 1984 and 1989 and marijuana use has declined from 9 percent to 8 percent, use of hard liquor has risen from 20 percent to 24 percent, and cocaine use has increased from about 1 percent to 2 percent. In reality, even the numbers showing a decline in usage of certain substances are not good news because they really represent a shift toward the more concentrated, more dangerous substances.

3. The *Des Moines Register* reported on December 2, 1989, that the Iowa State University Social and Behavioral Research Center for Rural Health found that 53 percent of rural Iowa youths ages twelve through seventeen consumed alcohol in the past year, compared with 44.6 percent nationwide. This gap was entirely accounted for by the Iowa girls, who outdrank those nationwide by 60 percent to 41 percent. This news followed findings reported in the February 6, 1989, *Des Moines Register* that cocaine use among Iowa teens was rising dramatically and that in 1987 more then 9 percent of fifteen- and sixteen-year old students in Iowa had tried some form of cocaine at least once. It seems that the "moral Midwest," where the popular perception is that family values prevail more than they do in other parts of the country, is experiencing one of the worst failures.

4. In 1987 the National Centers for Disease Control after sampling 11,000 eighth and tenth graders, reported that "about one in three has seriously contemplated suicide." The National Center for Health Statistics reported that in 1983 suicide was the second leading cause of death for persons aged fifteen to nineteen years of age. *Who's Who Among American High School Students* reported in a recent survey that 31 percent of the top high school juniors had considered suicide and 4 percent had tried it.

5. *The Wall Street Journal* reported on February 3, 1989, that "the number of Americans between the ages of ten and nineteen discharged from psychiatric units between 1980 and 1987 ballooned 43 percent," while "the population of that age group shrank 11 percent during that period." The opinion of experts cited in this article is: "Family turmoil—divorce, remarriage, frequent migration—and two-career households have left many parents either too busy or too distracted to deal with adolescents."

6. A Lou Harris poll reported in the February 1988 *Redbook* found that nationwide 4 percent of twelve-year olds, 10 percent of thirteen-year olds, 20 percent of fourteen-year olds, 29 percent of fifteen-year olds, and 46 percent of sixteen-year olds have had sexual intercourse. Few of those sexually active children use birth control—evidence of the ineffectiveness of sex education efforts. The article reflects the same level of ignorance among young people about sex as existed before all the efforts to provide information. One of the results of this is the soaring rate of teenage pregnancies. The extensive anti-AIDS campaign for "Safe Sex" has also had little impact: two thirds of sexually active teens take no precautions.

7. *Time*, February 1990, reported that American thirteen-year-olds were last internationally in math and "nearly last in science." The arti-

---

What?—Me—Learn?

Reports abound on the failure of the educational process. Children are graduating from school unable to do simple arithmetic, read, write, or balance a checkbook. They are unable to find their own state on a map or the United States on the world map. Many don't know who George Washington was, who is the vice-president of our country, how to vote, or how to fill out a job application form. Test scores reflecting college readiness have declined.

With many of our young in a state of real ignorance about their society, why should we be surprised that they do not behave as we think they should? Why should we be surprised that they seem incapable of working in their own interests? In the case of many children, it is as though they had dropped from sight, dropped from membership in society.

cle further stated that 84 percent of Americans attain "a high school diploma or its equivalent" *by age twenty-four*. This means that one in six does not even have the *equivalent* of a high school education by age twenty-four.

The Streetwise Child

The term "streetwise" is a popular term frequently used to describe those youth who have taken to living all or a major part of the time "on the street." Actually, few of them live literally "on the street." They live in abandoned houses, garages, or under bridges. A large number live with young adults who are living on some kind of welfare or are only marginally employed. Many are provided beds in return for sexual services, running drugs or, engaging in other illegal activities.

Somehow, the term "streetwise" has acquired an aura of glamour, even among adults. For many young people, it has become rather a compliment to be known as "streetwise." Children in increasing numbers are choosing the "street" life-style: living nowhere in particular, having no plans or goals, forming no lasting relationships, learning no legitimate marketable skills.

There are a number of reasons for this mass-runaway phenomenon. First, many of these children have plenty to run away from (physical or sexual abuse, alcoholic parents, or emotional abuse). Some children simply become fed up, believing, often correctly, that anything is better than staying in their impossible family situation. One of the authors has talked with many teenage boys and girls who "got beat up one time too many," or who "got tired of fighting off my dad and brothers wanting sex all the time." These are children who may be at least as well off on their own as they would be at home. Finding little help available, they often head for the "street."

Second, the "street" can sustain them. Not all who run away are from hopeless home situations. Some children who might otherwise make an effort to work things out at home find it entirely too easy to simply leave and survive on the street. Children are often able to beg and scrounge enough to get by for many days at a time. Old buildings are available for shelter, along with housing furnished by unscrupulous or foolish adults. The "system" can often be successfully "worked" for temporary shelter, food, and clothing. Services do exist, some of them excellent, to help kids who want to select an alternative to street life or to return home. Far fewer children will take advantage of this than could. There are plenty of attractive, easy opportunities for illegal activities: theft, drug running, burglary, picking pockets, stealing purses, even mugging. And there are always exploitive adults standing ready to benefit from highly marketable attractiveness of teenage and child prostitutes.

Third, the choice is there to be made. The legal system of adult society no longer really prohibits running away. During the middle 1970s, there was a nationwide fervor to "decriminalize" running away from home. The well-meaning cry was raised that "these children don't need to be locked up, they need us to love them!" This movement was so successful that it is now impossible to hold a child against his or her will unless a serious crime has been committed or unless the child can be diagnosed as seriously mentally ill. National and state statutes clearly spell out that doors cannot be locked on runaway children.

Characteristics of the Streetwise Child

Streetwise and malnourished.
Streetwise and begging on the corner.
Streetwise and pregnant.
Streetwise and selling their bodies.
Streetwise and have scabies.
Streetwise and committing criminal acts.
Streetwise and addicted to cocaine or alcohol.
Streetwise and can't add, subtract, multiply, or read.
Streetwise and infected with syphilis.
Streetwise and exploited.
Streetwise and dying.

We believe that the most accurate descriptive term for this phenomenon is not "streetwise," but "street stupid." Indeed, as the cry was raised in the seventies, "these children need us to love them."

If we love them, then why do we let them live on the street?

If we love them, then why do they want to live on the street?

Here is one of the clearest examples of the need for tough-minded love—a love that expects; a love that leads; a love that gives and rewards giving; a love that knows when to insist, when to request, and how to forgive.

The Single Parent

The single parent is a fact of our times. Many women are raising children without marrying. Other parents are divorced. Some find themselves alone due to the death of a spouse. In 1970 only 15 percent of American children lived in single parent homes; by 1980 this was up to 23 percent; now it is variously estimated that 30 to 35 percent of American children are in single-parent homes.

The proportion of our children being raised by single parents is clearly high and rapidly climbing. There is a good deal of hand-wringing about this, with worry constantly being expressed over the effects of single parenting. Public figures ranging from mental health practitioners to politicians to preachers remind us daily of the "dangers" of this single-parenting trend.

The hand-wringers may have a point, but what purpose is being served by all this loud concern? True, there is little doubt that raising children alone is much more difficult than with the help of a marriage partner. Most of the time, children grow better when raised by two parents than by only one. The important fact, however, is that an increasing number of children will be raised by single parents, resulting in this challenge: How can we best equip all parents, married and single, to give their children a good start in life?

We need also to remember that some single parents *can* overcome this obstacle and do a good job of raising children. Everyone of us knows at least one example of a single parent who has done it or is doing so. While parenting is a task usually better done if shared with a loving, helping, competent partner, we all know that some single people, both men and women, have done it alone and have done it well.

At the same time, some two-parent families are clearly incompetent to raise emotionally whole children, and the results can be sad and tragic. Often these parents cannot succeed even with professional assistance. A very large portion of the young persons described as "streetwise" are from two-parent families. While the odds are better for the child with two parents at home, it is no guarantee. There are people who simply have not acquired the capability to succeed as parents and could not succeed if they numbered a dozen to a family, let alone two.

For Family Discussion

While two good parents may be better than one, the controlling factor that determines success in parenting is not the *number* of parents, but their *quality*.
1. What does "quality" mean?
2. Is "quality" really more important than numbers?
3. What does the "quality of a parent" refer to?
4. What qualities are good in a parent?
5. How does quality relate to other areas of life?

A Tale of Two Nations

It is a central tenet of the tough-minded philosophy that the only competition that works is competition with yourself. This is true of nations, teams, or individuals. One of the great challenges of parenting is to instill this in our children. We truly diminish our possibilities when we compete with others; we truly enhance them when we compete with ourselves.

We believe that the success of any nation will ultimately be determined by the strength of its most basic institution—*the family*. Yet, nations often seem to be unaware of this, pouring effort instead into grandiose schemes and repeating the same old mistakes. Let's take a look at two nations, and the families within them, as examples of how two very different cultures can be making the same mistake, in almost opposite-appearing ways!

The American public in recent years keeps hearing about the new "Japanese Peril." The American people are continually told that we must out-work, out-wit, out-invent, out-produce, out-compete and in every way out-do Japan.

As with many over-statements, there is some truth in this. Our position of world leadership, our prosperity, our welfare, even our continued independence can be lost to a vigorous nation like Japan. This has happened many times throughout history. But *it doesn't have to be that way*! We have these things because they were earned, and they are things that can be earned anew by every generation. If each generation is up to it, our success is assured.

It is only through seeking and developing strength from within ourselves that our nation, or any nation, can have a successful future. In the final analysis we and the Japanese, and every other people on earth, face the same challenge. For a nation, strength from within is generated in its families.

It has been said that once in each generation every nation faces the threat of destruction at the hands of a new invasion of barbarians—its own children. This view has an element of truth in that each generation surely has the potential to become an alienated and destructive force, uncommitted to the ideals of the culture. When this occurs within a nation, then, historically, that nation disappears from the scene. It is, however, equally true that each new generation has the potential for greatness beyond anything that nation has ever before achieved. History equally bears out both of these possibilities.

What is it that assures the quality of each generation? What determines a generation's potential for success? Is it good schools? Is it good nourishment? Is it quality medical care? At the end of World War II, there were entire nations in which all of these had been destroyed, but many of those nations rose quickly to re-emerge in highly successful ways. The basis of their ability to produce a new and vigorous generation lay in the strength of the most fundamental institution in the human world, the family. The values and attitudes instilled in their children by strong families assured those nations' revival and success.

The Japanese Family—Also In Trouble

Our focus in *Tough-Minded Parenting* is to enhance the family—to teach values that are life-giving tools to our children. We have cited the increasing evidence of the potential failure of the American family to produce a generation that will be able to maintain our present quality

---

How Firm a Foundation

While this central theme of common sense really needs no validation, it often has been expressed well enough to bear repeating here.

Virginia Satir states in her classic parenting book *People Making*, "The family is the 'factory' where this kind of person is made."

Carl Jung in *The Theory of Psychoanalysis* states: "The little world of childhood with its familiar surroundings is a model of the greater world. The more intensively a family has stamped its character upon the child, the more it will tend to feel and see its miniature world again in the bigger world of adult life."

Mang Tze, about 300 years B.C., observed: "The root of the kingdom is in the state. The root of the state is in the family. The root of the family is in the person of its head."

---

of life, let alone achieve new greatness. Are we alone in facing this problem?

Seemingly not. Jon Woronoff, in his 1985 book, *Japan: The Coming Social Crisis*, points out that there are serious signs of failure to adequately prepare young Japanese for life. He states: "violence is breaking out in the schools, as older students victimize the younger ones and even insult and beat up the teachers." Woronoff found an ever-increasing number of juveniles involved in criminal offenses, although these were nothing approaching the numbers in the U.S. The significant point is that the trend is upward.

Woronoff also states that the number of suicides in the under-14 group doubled in the ten years previous to 1985. With suicide already a tradition in Japan, and overall Japanese rates already higher than in the United States, most experts worry that the number of suicides among Japanese children could reach very high proportions.

Woronoff also observes that the increasing obsession of the head of the household with business is leading to trouble in the Japanese family. Because of the increasing absence of the father from the home, there is coming to be a role conflict between the traditional superior male role and the necessity that the mother assume the controlling role in the home. Thus there is confusion between what the boy is told the man is to be and what he actually observes happening in the home. What is the truth about what a man is to be?

How confusing to the daughters as well, observing their mother playing the dominant role at home while being taught the opposite! What is the truth about what a lady is to be?

One of the authors, having traveled and lectured in Japan, observed that it is a social requirement that the husband spend several hours each evening drinking with other men in business. The husband then often comes home late, inebriated, and incapable of entering into family life. One executive said, "My children's principal impression of me is that of a drunk, exhausted person." This time spent away from home and ineffectiveness when at home further alienates the father from the wife and children and further weakens the children's understanding of proper values.

Dr. Lyla Maynard, who heads the Department of Child Development at the Des Moines Area Community College, Ankeny, Iowa, recently spent several months as a guest of the Japanese government engaged in on-site study of Japanese child-rearing practices, with particular interes. in factors leading to the high rate of suicide among children. Her observations included:

"All of the responsibility for child rearing rests on the Japanese mother, who determines early in the child's life what will be the life goal for the child. The mother then determines a strategy for attaining that goal, and lays out a complete life plan of education and work for the child all compulsively aimed at attaining the child's goal.

"The mother arranges for the child to attend the schools most likely to help that child become whatever it is that she has determined he/she should become. Included in this school plan is the "Juku," or "after school/school," in which the child must be enrolled to assure the necessary competitive edge. Hence, the child spends the day striving for perfection in the regular school, then spends extra hours preparing for the critical examinations yet to come. The honor of the family is at stake; the child's very reason for existence is at stake.

"At about age eighteen, there is a very important college entrance examination; there are no second chances for this. If the child fails, there is little else for him to do, since substitute or secondary goals are culturally discouraged. It is perhaps no surprise that the age group of eighteen to nineteen has the second highest suicide rate in the nation.

"In addition, suicide is rising among the children. Those who seem not to be in conformity or not achieving, and who feel that they are unable to conform or achieve as expected, have no one to turn to, no alternatives, no hope, and no reason to live.

"Even for the youngest children, the pressure to conform and to attain 100 percent perfection is tremendous. The shame resulting from failing to do so is so great that many children take the suicide way out as the only acceptable escape from shame."

Faced with conflicting and uncompromising expectations in the home and from the business society, and with increasing resistance on the part of the youth, Japanese parenting is said by many to be in as much trouble, although for different reasons, as is parenting in the United States. In spite of this, the reaction seems to be to increase, rather than decrease, pressure to fit the mold absolutely—and to intensify the ideology that the individual is important only insofar as he or she meets expectations externally derived from, and imposed by, the group. The child is to be *repressed, compressed, suppressed,* and *depressed*—all words that contain the word *press,* the prefix for *pressure.* This flies in the face of the enhancing, lifting, and expanding approach of tough-minded parenting.

More of the Same

It appears that the responses by Japan, the United States, and other nations to their failures with young people may have another element in common: we are all making the same mistake—trying more of the same solution that has been unsuccessfully applied in the past.

The traditional response to social problems in the United States has been to try to "educate" our way out of it. The assumption is that if only people are provided with enough information, they will make the right choices. There is a powerful pressure to "mind our own business" when it comes to moral behaviors and a belief that deviant behavior is simply based on a lack of factual information. "Fill in the information gap," we

Expecting the Best

One of the central themes of this book is to "expect the best of yourself and your children." The authors feel that this is an element that is largely missing and misunderstood in families today. This is true for different reasons and in different ways not only in the United States and Japan but throughout the world.

An integral part of expecting the best involves the discovery of the best that is within you and your child and the development of the skills to produce that best. This does not mean trying for perfection. It is definitely not the same as the 100 percent, lockstep, unbending conformity with the externally imposed expectations characteristic of Japan. Neither is it the same as the vagueness, hesitancy, uncertainty, and avoidance of expectations that is characteristic of American families.

We will show that when parents internally inspire excellent expectations for themselves and their children, within a framework of love, values, vision, and candid communication, the best is what results. Excellent parents are thus like a compass, providing direction and magnetic pull.

Expectations and Self Image

Externally Imposed Expectations	Unclearly Defined Expectations	Internally Deprived Expectations
(Japanese Model)	(American Model)	Tough-Minded Model)

reason, "and people will do what is best for them." Americans act as though ignoring profanity and obscenity, will cause them to go away. When parents do this, what do children conclude is "right"?

This belief is extended to the imparting of basic life skills, such as decision making. "Show the kids how to reason their way through the choices they are confronted with," goes the logic, "and they will make the right choices for themselves." All of the emphasis is on the how, when what young people really need to know is why!

The "just say no" movement rests on the same idea. It is true that the impact of the "just say no" campaign, though limited, was very real and very positive. However, it had an impact largely because the campaign imparted a feeling that there was moral support from the larger society for saying no, not because children were learning for the first time how to say it.

How have you heard such statements as: "Show children what drugs and alcohol are all about, and the possible consequences of using them. Show them what sex is all about, and the possible consequences of sexual activity. Provide them with complete information about the worth of an education. Give them information! Then they will make good choices." This can be heard at any conference for educators, social workers, and parents. It can be read in numerous published materials aimed at fighting deviancy in youth.

These are the same approaches we have been using for at least the past three decades. And now, faced with increasing evidence of the failure of past approaches, our response seems to be—more of the same.

Information alone does not change behavior; it does not create moti-

---

The term "tough-minded" refers to a quality of quiet, confident resilient strength that enables the person who exemplifies it to lead others to become the best they can possibly be. When practiced in the business world, it has led to high productivity, motivation, and enhanced satisfaction for both the team and the consumer. The tough-minded person loves life, builds people, is excited about starting each day, is an actualizer! The authors have enthusiastically welcomed the challenge of applying this concept to meeting the greatest need present in the world today: that of parenting our children.

vation; it does not provide passion; it does not inspire desire. Preachments without example are actually counterproductive.

Action, change, motivation, passion, and desire are based on such experiences as giving and receiving love; acquiring goals, vision and hope for the future; creating clear expectations; building a self-image of being worthy, unique, capable, and wanted; and, throughout all of this, developing a strong attachment to positive values.

Building Stronger Families

Building stronger, value-led families is the only answer to this trouble. We must strengthen our families, ourselves, and our children from within.

3

The Pledge of the Tough-Minded Parent

On my honor as a parent, I will do my best:

To expect the best from myself and my children.

To share love, laughter, and life with my children.

To develop and be guided by the highest vision and values.

To be truthful and honest with my children at all times.

To teach and lead by my example.

To encourage my children to share fully in our lives together.

To accept my children enthusiastically and vulnerably.

To find and develop the strengths in every family member.

To change yelling, telling, and commanding to asking, listening, and hearing.

To demonstrate a clear link between expectations, performance, and outcomes.

For Family Discussion

Here are dictionary definitions of the word *pledge*:

"A binding promise or agreement."

"Something of value given as security for the performance of an act."

"To offer solemnly, as one's honor or word, as security."

1. What is being promised in the "Pledge of the Tough-Minded Parent"?
2. What does "honor" mean?
3. Can a person lose honor? Can a person regain it? How?
4. What "something of value given as security" is at risk in giving this pledge?

This pledge is a system of values for children and parents. We urge parents to copy and post the Pledge, to refer to it often, and to discuss it with your children on a regular basis.

Here are brief explanations of the ten points.

On My Honor As a Parent I Will Do My Best

It is no accident that the Pledge begins with the familiar line: "On my honor." It is an honor to be a parent; it is a privilege that most of those who are denied the experience envy. Parenting is not a right, it is a calling! Parents have been given the greatest trust granted to human beings: the responsibility for guiding a child toward his or her full human potential.

"Honor" also means the giving of one's word, a promise not to be given lightly. It means "I will do this thing that I say that I will do."

It is not uncommon to hear of parents risking or even sacrificing their own lives for the protection of their children. Parents are often known to donate their kidneys, leap in front of traffic, or enter burning structures to save their children. Most parents do not think twice about "doing their best" to save the life of their child. And that is what is at stake all along the line: the life of your child is possibly more at risk from failure to be equipped with good values and a good example than from entering swift water without swimming skills or from failure to be vaccinated against disease.

1. "To expect the best of myself and my children."

Think for a moment of the best parents you know. What do they expect of their children? What do their children deliver? Is it not also true that these same parents expect great things of themselves?

What is the best? How do you know when someone is giving their best? It may be hard to tell whether someone, even your own child, is truly giving his best, but you can't fool yourself; you always know whether you are giving your best. The only way to get the best from others is first to be the best moral example, the best performance example, the best loving example, the best self-disciplined example that you can. Only then can you expect others to give their best.

Expecting the best is often confused with expecting perfection. Perfectionism sets us up for failure. "The best" accepts human error and individual capabilities and is attained when you are competing against yourself, not some outside standard. We define excellence as: "giving a thing your best shot, and knowing it." If you expect the best, encourage the best, reward the best, then most of the time you will get it. Certainly you will get much more than if you expect anything else.

2. To share love, laughter and life with my children.

It feels good to share love, laughter and life with your children. It just makes good sense! How else can they know you? How else can they follow the example you provide? Why else would they want to? How else can they know who you are? How better can they understand how you approach problems than to share in your experience of doing so?

A person who is loved at home does not need to seek proof elsewhere that they can be loved! Children who have plenty of fun at home have less incentive to seek substitutes elsewhere. Children who have good fun at home will look for and be able to enjoy good fun elsewhere.

For Family Discussion

What are the key words in this statement?
Children who share in the life of their parent will find life to be a familiar friend.

---

3. To develop and be guided by the highest faith, vision and values.

Most parents want their children to be better people and more successful than they were themselves. This is a normal feeling, but the question is, How do we measure success? We want our children to have life goals to strive for, and we want those goals to be noble aims that both we and the child can be proud of.

How can you assure that your children will have noble values and goals? As in all other instances, your child will be guided by your example and your integrity. Define a noble set of action goals for yourself and base them on the highest standard of faith and values you can define.

Be clear as to your own personal, spiritual faith—those things you believe without question to be true—and discuss your faith with your children. Show them how you have drawn from this your life's meaning and the values that you follow. Share with them how your goals are connected to these beliefs.

It does not matter whether your child shares precisely your goals; what does matter is that your child's goals will likely be similar in value and nobility to your own. The example you are providing, and the standard of performance you expect of yourself, is that of living by your values.

To expect the best, you must have a vision of the best. One of the best ways for families to do this is to develop a Family Mission Statement. (See Appendix A for Steven Covey's guide to developing a Family Mission Statement.) Many individuals also develop personal mission statements. It might be helpful a parent to do this before working on one for the family.

4. To be truthful and honest with my children.

It is possible to be truthful in a technical sense without being honest. Our society has developed to a high degree the techniques for making statements that are legally true but which actually convey a lie or conceal the truth.

Children are hard to fool! Children often know when they are hearing the truth and when they are not. One of the biggest mistakes a parent can make is to underestimate the ability of their children to detect a lie. The most underestimated lie detectors in the world are children.

For Family Discussion

People need truthful and honest evaluation and praise.

1. How can you really know what another thinks of your performance?

2. What if you are never sure that others are giving honest praise?

3. Can you know when you have truly done well if you never hear an honest suggestion as to what might have been better?

4. Can anyone benefit from the praise of a known liar?

5. What does it mean to be honest with yourself?

6. What does it mean to say of laws that "The letter killeth, but the spirit giveth life" (2 Cor. 3:6, KJV)?

Children respect and appreciate the truth. They can handle a realistic promise that falls short of what they want better than the discovery that they have been promised something when there was no possibility or intent to deliver it.

5. To teach and lead by my example.

The best teachers live what they are trying to teach! The best leader is one who sets a reasonable pace, demanding of self what is demanded of the troops. The leader is at the head showing the way, guiding and pulling the young ones along by the power and inspiration of example. This achieves much more than trying to get behind and push!

How many times have you heard someone say to a child, "Do what I say, not what I do"? What a useless admonition! What a waste of breath! We "sophisticated" adults, knowing the "ways of the world," judge each other on the basis of what we see being done and pretty much ignore what is said if it is different from our own observations. Do we, then, think that our children are different?

Children will do what we do! We must lead them in the way by our example.

6. To encourage my children *to share fully* in our lives together.

Families all encounter a wide range of both successes and crises.

Children are thus prepared for their own crises and successes as adults by what they have learned while growing up. They must learn how to enjoy the times when things go well and how to deal with the disappointments when things don't go well. Parents who fully share all of these events with the children as they happen not only prepare them for their own life but can actually derive strength from the children as well.

"Involvement precedes commitment" is a familiar, well-proven rule in group leadership. Give children a voice in family affairs. While a voice is not necessarily an equal vote, it is a chance for a respectful hearing of everyone's opinions, wants, and needs.

7. "To accept my children *enthusiastically and vulnerably.*"

Take joy in who your children *are*; enjoyment of what they *do* will follow naturally. Express that joy! Approach individual and family tasks and pleasures with gusto. Enthusiasm is the reflection of expecting the best.

For Family Discussion

Celebrating Your Childrens' Accomplishments
This is one of the great guidelines in successful families.
• Share in your childrens' victories, large and small.
• Let them know what you think of them as a person.
• Attend their school and church programs, recitals, or other occasions.
• Take pictures and recordings.
• Express your approval and appreciation.
• Praise who they are even more than what they have done.
• Make birthdays a major occasion, focusing on another year of growth in the life of a very important person.

The celebrating of your childrens' achievements is not just a "cute little concession"; it is a recognition of real achievement, and it will lead to more of the same.

To be tough-minded is, among other qualities, to be emotionally vulnerable. Tough-minded parents can say "I'm sorry" without diminishing their self-image. The tough mind and the tender heart are one.

Everyone makes mistakes; parents need not hesitate to admit them. Everyone feels pain, hurt, and fear; everyone needs to be able to express it. Parents will find that when they expose their feelings to their children there is nothing to fear. Everyone accidentally does things that turn out to be ridiculous or humorous. Parents need to be able to laugh at themselves, and to enjoy having their children laugh with them.

8. "To find and develop the strengths in every family member."

View yourself and your family members as bundles of strengths. Develop a habit of defining family members and yourself in terms of strengths and value. Look at so-called weaknesses as merely strengths that are missing or that need developing.

This positive view of self will lead to gratitude for the strengths you have. It will lead your children to be grateful for the strengths they have. They can then learn to be grateful for who they are rather than dissatisfied with who they are not. This is the essential element in learning to love yourself.

Respect is essential to love. Have you ever loved anyone that you did not first respect? Strength is respected. If you and your children are in the habit of thinking of self in terms of strengths, self-respect will follow. Trying to gain respect through deviant action then becomes unnecessary. A healthy love for self is based on existing and developing strengths.

Once the habit of building on strengths is established, there is no end to it. This can be a zestful habit throughout life.

9. "To change yelling, telling, and commanding to asking, listening, and hearing."

We often seem to believe that if we say something loud enough, someone will listen. Depending on a loud voice to gain attention is a device of short-term usefulness at best. Children quickly learn to tune this out.

We also seem to place a high value on "telling," and want to project an image of being "one who tells others." How many conversations have you heard in which an event is being recounted by the person who says, "So I *told* him . . ." followed by a story that is usually a little overstated? How many times have you believed these stories? How many times have *you* used this same words?

Do You Hear Me?

This often-employed device has found its way into the monologues of a number of comedians—and with good reason. It's so ridiculous that it's funny. The parent discovers the child doing something against instructions, becomes very angry, and loudly harangues the child for several minutes at a close distance, and closes with the ridiculous question, "Do you hear me?" Of course! The child would have to be deaf not to have heard under those circumstances.

The real question is, does a child truly hear when being yelled at?

Telling is neither instructing nor communicating. Telling is not respecting, and it engenders no respect. Telling does not result in performance at the level of best expectations. It diminishes the dignity both of the teller and the "tellee."

Behavior simply does not change unless the dignity of the person is enhanced, and this is done by asking and leading. Commanding is also of limited use in a family, although there are some occasional emergency situations in which a parent must be able to issue a command and be sure that the child will respond immediately. Every parent has experienced the terrifying moment when the toddler dashed into the street or other dangerous place, or reached for something dangerous, when distance made intervention in time impossible. For a young child, the commands "stop!" and "no!" should be used sparingly, but when they are used the child must be taught to respond right away for reasons of safety.

Children will respond to these rare emergency commands—if they respect the commander and are able to recognize that the command is something special calling for immediate obedience. If, however, commands are the common mode of conveying expectations, they will fail when they are truly needed. They will not convey special urgency and importance.

When you talk to your children, you hope to be listened to and you hope to be truly heard. Children hope for and need the same. You hope that your children will want to ask you about the matters of life that they need to know. If you set an example as the pattern for communication in the family, of asking, listening, and truly hearing them, your expectations will be communicated far more effectively then through any yelling, telling or commanding. Children hear you because they know that you will hear them.

10. "To demonstrate a clear link between expectations, performance, and outcomes."

There is, in the real world in which our children must ultimately make their way, a clear link between performance and outcomes. Essentially, you do get what you pay for—not more. You do, in the long run, receive according to your efforts. What better favor can you do your children than to prepare them for that truth?

Negative consequences for many of our actions are also in the real world. There are many children who have not experienced these truths at home. They are often unpleasantly surprised when they finally learn from real consequences.

Parents can help their children see the link between expectations and outcomes by providing rewards only when they are actually deserved. And the rewards should be provided *graciously and enthusiastically.* Parents can also help by using attention-getting responses, such as "time out" or "grounding," when a child seriously "tests" the boundaries or engages in a potentially harmful act. This lets children understand that there are negative consequences for their negative actions.

Demonstrating the link between expectations, performance, and outcomes is true child discipline.

The Good News

Tough-minded parenting is an adventure. It works! It's been tried before—*millions of times.* Lots of today's parents qualify as "tough-minded parents." It will work for *you.*

Tough-Minded parenting is good news.

Are you ready?

4

Who Are You Really?

Few things in life are tougher than being honest with yourself—and none is more vitally important. There are lots of familiar and convenient excuses for avoiding a clear-eyed insightful look at ourselves:

"*You* didn't understand when I said. . . ."

"But, I *told* you. . . ."

"You're always misunderstanding me. . . ."

Strengths: The Only Reality

It's hard to face the fact that how we look at ourselves determines how we perceive others. What do you see in you? Do you perceive yourself as a walking bundle of strengths? Or do you see yourself as a walking bundle of weaknesses?

What are strengths? First, it is crucial to realize that strengths are the only reality in anyone! What we mistakenly call weaknesses in a person are only insufficiently developed strengths. Strengths, in our tough-minded lexicon, are defined as: All the qualities, abilities, skills, and knowledge you have which enable you to be and do. They are the true realities in all things. Conversely, weaknesses are only what is absent or lacking. Strengths are our only building blocks—they are the only resources we can employ in every dimension of life. Strengths are the integrators of our lives, making the parts work as a unified whole. Thus, the meaning of *strength* and *integrity* is the same.

Expecting, Trying, Failing, and Growing Strong

Strengths are built by expecting the best of ourselves as human beings. This means not merely expecting the best of ourselves as students,

60

employees, athletes, or citizens, but as human beings—doing the best we can do in the areas of understanding, love, listening, and enjoying life.

At this point it is important to emphasize that expecting the best and expecting perfection are very different. This is especially vital for us as parents. When we are focusing on the strengths of our children, it is crucial that we accept them as who they are, and accept their mistakes and failures as part of them. To do this, we must be willing to recognize that mistakes and failures are a part of our own experience. We learn, grow, and gain strength by taking risks, making mistakes, and even failing.

Errare humanum est [To err is human].—Anonymous Latin Saying

To err is human, to forgive divine.—Alexander Pope.

Failing! So many parents feel threatened when their children fail. Taking it personally, parents may say things like:

"You didn't try hard enough!"

"If only you had . . ."

"What will people think?"

"Why didn't you . . . ?"

"I was embarrassed when you . . ."

"What's wrong with you?"

Failing is necessary to all progress. When we fail, we fail forward, learning from that failure.

One of the toughest, yet most important challenges for parents is to love children enough to let them make mistakes, to let them have failures, but to be there for them with unconditional love when they do. All human beings make errors in judgment, actions, words, thoughts, and behavior.

We all make mistakes in parenting. Parents are not *always* going to say and do the right thing or provide the right example. Sometimes parents are the ones responsible for family strife. The human temptation is to point fingers and try to justify or deny mistakes. A parent needs to be vulnerable, to apologize when appropriate, to be confident enough to take responsibility for mistakes, and to honestly let children know, *"I goofed!"* Our ability to do this begins with knowing, accepting, and loving ourselves.

Good parenting begins with parents. If children are able to see us, as parents, accepting our own mistakes, learning from them, and going on with life, they will learn to do the same. If, however, they see us *avoiding* responsibility, then they will surely learn to do that, too!

Sheltered

Parental fears for our children are quite normal. We often want to protect our children from every conceivable harm. What happens when we do this? Consider the hot-house plant, raised in a greenhouse, never experiencing wind or draft or stress. When that plant is taken out into the stress of the real world, it often dies.

What happens to the child who is artificially protected the same way?

Tough-minded parenting involves learning when and how to turn apparent stumbling blocks into stepping-stones. It all begins with how those stones are seen, either they are rocks that block the way or they are materials for paving the way.

R.L. Sharpe said:

> Isn't it strange
> That princes and kings,
> And clowns that caper
> In sawdust rings,
> And common people,
> Like you and me,
> Are builders for eternity?
>
> Each is given a bag of tools,
> A shapeless mass,
> A book of rules,
> And each must make,
> E're life has flown,
> A stumbling-block
> Or a stepping-stone.

Our strengths are our tools.—Our ability to assess the reality of our children, to truly come to know them, will depend directly on our ability to first know ourselves. A zestful, buoyant, and confident search for our own strengths, a lifelong quest, will steadily yield new insights into the present and potential strengths of our children. When we accomplish this significant, even dramatic, shift in focus, we can begin to learn who our children really are. However, if we are not making progress in learning who we are, it will be impossible to help our children learn who they are, what their strengths are, and what their best really is.

Building the Family Strength Bank

Creation of a "family strength bank" for families who seek greater cohesiveness, unity, and just plain joyfulness as a fully functioning unit, promises to be a major breakthrough for the near future. To understand how to do this, some new terms and definitions are needed:

1. A person's *strength* is a quality, ability, skill, or area of knowledge.
2. A family's *assests* are the individual strengths which are discovered and brought into play or put into action.
3. Its *liabilities* are its missing strengths.
4. A family's *capital* is the sum of the strengths of its members.
5. *Investments* are made by discovering, communicating, and developing strengths in the members of the family.

At H.O.P.E. we provide an assortment of strength discovery and strength building tools and games. One approach is to sit down together and mention every strength each person currently sees in the others, making sure that no references of any kind are made to "weaknesses."

(H.O.P.E. is a part of the Batten Foundation in Des Moines, Iowa. We work with people who are caught in the effects of substance abuse and addiction, whether they or some one else is the abuser. We work with families, schools, corporations, and government to develop programs, policies, and cultural climate changes to help prevent the abuse of alcohol and drugs, to mitigate its effects, and to prevent the onset or continuation of primary addiction.

Our present efforts include support groups for high school adolescents, a first-offender drunk driving treatment and education program, parenting seminars, work with adoptive situations, and work with divorcing families engaged in child custody disputes.)

Family strength-building sessions can be held on a regular basis. This may happen around the dinner table once a week. Each child and parent may be encouraged to tell of a new personal strength discovered in themselves. Following this, each may have the chance to tell each of the other family members of a new strength they see in that person. All such strengths are entered or deposited in the family strength bank.

A ledger may be set up to record and chronicle the individual and group strengths of the family. This can take the form of an attractively designed notebook labeled "Our Family Strength Bank." We make deposits in our family strength bank when we seek, identify, mention, and relate to the strengths of others. We enter each of these in the ledger.

What happens? Strength deposits can and will earn interest through mutual support of the investments. They will actually multiply and become greater than their sum. Everyone is multiply enriched!

This new family model can also form a basis to guide major family decisions, assignments, and projects.

Using Strengths to Achieve Individual and Family Goals

When all decisions, requests, and interpersonal actions are centered around this model, many good changes begin to happen in the family. They include such transitions from negative ways of approaching life to positive ways as those shown in the illustration "Reversing the G Forces."

"G Forces," as used in the illustration is like the figurative pull of gravity. Real gravity, of course, is necessary to keep us on this planet, and so it is not altogether a bad thing. Still, gravity works against much of what we try to do. The "G Forces" we are talking about here are those negative forces from the past, such as fearful, passive, and self-defeating attitudes and practices that retard and even reverse growth and forward movement. Transition to the positive forces of the future can release our potential for the future and allow us to grow and be-

REVERSING THE "G's"

POSITIVE 'G' FORCES of the FUTURE

- Expects the Best
- Focused and Laser-Like
- Optimistic
- Pulls
- Flexible
- Open-Minded
- Go-Giver
- Love, Faith, Hope
- Confident and Growing
- Expective
- Result-Focused
- Unsatisfied
- Macro Thinker
- Open and Vulnerable
- Explosive
- Quality-Oriented
- Loyal
- Expansive and Growing
- Cares and Acts
- Result-Focused
- Open-Minded
- Loves Change
- Pro-Active
- Open-Minded
- Integrity
- Pulls
- Focused, Laser-Like
- Tough Mentally, Physically
- Lifts Others Up

GRATITUDE

NEGATIVE 'G' FORCES of the PAST

- Diminishes Others
- Selfish
- Diffused
- Pushes
- Expedient
- Cynical and Doubting
- Reactive
- Quits Easily
- Closed-Minded
- Resists Change
- Depressed and Diffident
- Disloyal
- Quantity-Oriented
- Implosive
- Defensive
- Micro-Thinker
- Dissatisfied
- Activity-Focused
- Directive
- Against
- Doubt/Fear
- Hate
- Go-Getter
- Timid
- Rigid
- Against
- Passive in Neutral
- Expects the Worst
- Evasive and Nice

come all we can be. When we apply this to the family, everyone will profit by new growth and change.

Along with building a family strength bank, each member of the family who is old enough can set up a personal strength notebook. This calls for entering in each notebook all the strengths identified by other family members and then attempting to add one new strength each week. Once established as a habit, this can literally go on for years and become an ongoing basis for both new personal strengths discoveries and a steady escalation of confidence and personal goals.

Expecting the Best from Yourself

All caring, thinking parents want their children to be positively motivated. Such parents want to provide an example of this for their children to follow. The key to positive personal motivation lies within you.

Here is an exercise that can help you discover some things about the best you can be. Please give careful thought to the following requests and questions and answer them thoughtfully.

Five of my inner strengths are:

_____

_____

_____

_____

_____

What would I be willing to do for someone I really care about?

_____

_____

Why do I feel it is important to really listen and hear what people say?

_____

_____

How do I feel about giving earned praise?

_____

_____

Am I doing all I can to help my family feel involved in family endeavors? Yes _____ No _____

Does my example communicate what I *think* it does? Yes _____ No _____

Does my example communicate what I *wish* it to? Yes _____
No _____

Do I relish the opportunity to provide positive reinforcement?
Yes _____ No _____

Do I need strength in my life? Yes _____ No _____

What does excellence mean to me?

_____

_____

How do I know I am doing my best?

_____

_____

Why is it important to do my best?

_____

_____

What happens when someone expects me to do my best?

_____

_____

What happens when I expect others to do their best?

_____

_____

What happens when someone expects my worst or second best?

_____

What positive G forces stimulate me the most?

_____

_____

Continue to provide room for stretch in your own life and in the lives of your family. You will be surprised to discover new and exciting things about who you are and can be. This, in turn, will make it possible for you to reach out and help others discover possibilities that will enable them to grow. One of the finest tributes you can give another person is to help them gain the ability to see who they are and who they can be.

Expecting the Best From You and From Them

Every day of the week vast numbers of children are rushed into deciding what to *do*. Woefully little time is spent on leading and pulling children into determining and understanding who and what to *be*.

When Your Children Look at You, What Do They See?

This	or	*This*
Passive permissiveness		Loving discipline
Rigid, unyielding demands		Loving Discipline
Too busy to listen		Time to hear
A "knower"		A "learner"
Conditional love		Unconditional love
Defensiveness		Vulnerability
Diminisher and shrinker		Stretcher and expander
Negativism		Positivism
Escapism or expedient		Pursuit of challenges
Focus on "impossibilities"		Focus on "possibilities"
Dissatisfied		Unsatisfied
Activity oriented		Goal oriented
Procrastination/compromise		Do your best
Cynicism		Openness and wonder
Griping		Gratitude
Giving Directions		Giving Direction
Despair		Hope
Sordidness and sloth		Truth and energy
Competing with others		Competing with self
Passive erosion		Passionate renewal
Sloppy and flabby		Pursues fitness
Expedient		Accountable
Dwells on weaknesses		Builds on strength
Telling, pushing, driving		Asking, listening, and hearing
Hard-minded		Tough-minded

When we know who and what we wish to be, we will find it relatively easy to know what to do.

One of our most fervent wishes is that parents will become committed to helping their children become all they can be.

The child who is fortunate enough to grow up in a loving family committed to help each other become all they can be runs much less risk of succumbing to drugs, suicide, or the other current dangers in our world.

Family life can be exciting, renewing, challenging, and fun.

The tough mind is the open, growing, supple, and resilient mind. Even though greatly oversimplified, the following acronym is useful in understanding what our *best* can *be*:

Being
Expectations
Strengths
Trust

Being—The here-and-now process of feeling, striving, hoping, reaching, and achieving.

Expectations—Claiming life's possibilities. It is possible to work out a comprehensive blueprint of expectations in virtually any family that *decides* to do this.

Strengths—The true realities in all things. Weaknesses are only what is absent or insufficient.

Trust—The feeling that expectations will be met. The implicit belief in the integrity or strength of the potential behavior of another person.

Do you care enough, to commit to becoming all you can be? Your family will benefit, and they will love you.

It is absolutely crucial to reemphasize that we are not advocating perfection. Such a goal puts us on a collision course with certain failure, and who needs that?

Rather, we recommend targeting excellence. We define excellence in the tough-minded lexicon as: giving an event or thing your best shot and knowing it.

Is there really any other choice?

5

Child Development: Growing in the Light

"To every thing there is a season, and a time to every purpose under heaven" (Eccl. 2:16).

"Thy word is a lamp unto my feet and a light unto my path" (Ps. 119: 105).

"It is circumstance and proper timing that give an action its character and make it either good or bad." Agesilaus, 444-400 BC, from Plutarch, *Lives*

The life history of any person is the unfolding of human potential. There is a clear order of events in this unfolding, especially in the early, or childhood, part of life.

A child's life moves quickly through time. During childhood a child must acquire literally millions of skills, words, ideas, actions, emotions, relationships, and values. The most important of these is the guiding light of a value system which the child will develop and use to make decisions.

Values are the most important tools you use in building your life. Like physical skills, vocabulary, learning of mathematics, or the growth of a relationship, a system of values grows little by little as the result of thousands of separate experiences. Values are developed as the child experiences life and makes choices along the way. The ability of children to find their way depends on the strength of this guiding light. Eventually, the light of their values may grow strong enough to truly illuminate their path, and even shed some light on the paths of others.

The Worlds of Childhood and Youth

A dictionary definitions of "world" is: "the sphere or scene of one's life and action." This definition reflects the fact that each of us lives quite

70

literally in a "world of our own," made up of the physical and social environment we perceive. The more growing children see positive behaviors in their world, the stronger are the values they develop to carry into adulthood.

We do not suggest that you can "program" your child like a computer and certainly do not suggest that you try to. Rather, we hope that, while providing a consistent anchor, you will relish the variability of your children. The aim is to lead rather than to control. The aim is to have influence over your children, not to have power but to *empower* your children to lead lives that you and they can be proud of.

"I shall light a candle of understanding in thine heart, which shall not be put out" (The Apocrypha, 2 Esdras 14:25).

Infancy

The bonds children form during infancy create the most influential lifetime relationships in the learning of values. To the infant, the world is

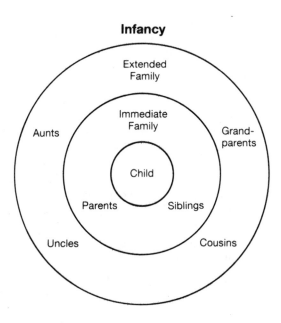

made up of a limited number of immediate persons, including the immediate family and certain regular caregivers that may be outside the family. This world principally includes the parent(s) and any brothers or sisters, but it may also include a regular babysitter and a weekly contact with a church teacher. (See diagram "Infancy.) These people are everything to

---

The Non-family Caretaker

In a growing number of homes, both parents desire to pursue careers. Ours society is achievement-oriented. We raise our children with the idea that they can learn skills, apply them in the real world, and they will then be rewarded personally and materially. Parenthood sometimes creates a conflict with these dreams.

Enter the baby-sitter and the day-care service. "Baby-sitter" is a term that is often applied to the care of children of all ages by someone other than the parent. In our society such care while parents are at work often begins at such an early age that the term applies quite literally. Children often enter the external world at a very early age, when they are, in fact, "babies." (See Diagram.)

The child in such a situation is in a daily state of transition from one milieu to another, and must make a daily adjustment. In some tribal societies, this would not be a problem, since all members of the tribe who might be caring for the child will have such similar values that consistency is not sacrificed. Our society, however, exhibits very diverse values, even within a small geographic range.

Parents need to keep in mind the "tribal" analogy when seeking out-of-home care for their children: Keep the care within your own "tribe of values" whenever possible.

If the babysitting service, relative's home or day care presents to the child similar language, similar surroundings, and most importantly of all, similar values, the transition will be less abrupt and the adjustment easier. Feel free as a parent to ask penetrating questions in these areas when selecting an out-of-home care service. The matter of religious views of the caretaker should be given careful thought, as there is a wide variety of messages delivered.

The child is not ready at an early age to cope with the differences in values and examples that the peer world has to offer. It makes sense to keep those differences to a minimum when the child is very small.

the baby. They are the baby's "world." On the outer edge of the infant's world is the extended family, grandparents, aunts, uncles, and cousins.

The task of the newborn is simply to be. Their job at first is simply to accept, then increasingly to seek and accept, nurturing and affection, with only their love and trust to offer in return.

Early Entry Into External Worlds

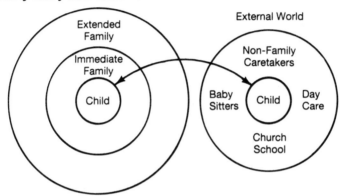

The transition adjustment is determined by the similarity of the persons, values and physical surroundings

Applying the Pledge

An infant can relate to *love, laughter and life* as well as a person can at any age. Babies are designed for this; it comes naturally.

This is the time to *live the example* of giving your unconditional love.

If your expectation of your baby is to smile, gurgle, squeal, and cry; then you are expecting the best they have to give. These are very significant achievements for a baby!

Share with your baby the pleasure of a smile; laughter; a soft voice; a firm, confident and gentle touch; the warmth of being held; the delightful infantile grasp of an adult finger.

Lead your baby to expect to be clean.

Accept your baby for simply being there, for simply being.

While babies cannot grasp anything as complicated as fully developed values, they learn who is trustworthy and affectionate to them. They are developing a relationship with those whom they will most closely imitate. They become increasingly aware of these people, who are usually their parents and siblings. They adjust to them. They develop specific responses to them.

Because having their needs met is the top priority to babies, they learn to act in ways that will cause the people who make up their world to act favorably toward them. This is their experimental beginning of imitative behavior.

Affirmation for Infants

I'm glad you are alive.
You belong here.
What you need is important to me.
You can grow at your own pace.
All of your feelings and reactions are all right.
I love you, and I care for you unconditionally.

There is often a lot of stress in being a new parent. Babies can't tell you what they want or need. Accept the fact that you will not always know what to do; it's all right to be uncertain. Ask your friends, family, or physician for advice.

Babies can try the patience of any parent. When the usual methods don't work and the baby still cries, a parent can become afraid and even angry. One thing that will not get babies to do what you want is intimidation: they cannot be intimidated because they cannot understand threats. A threat is something that is going to happen in the future, and they have no concept of future yet. The only result is more stress for everyone. In spite of your anger or fear, providing them with love and acceptance will meet their needs and bring about peace and quiet sooner than any other approach.

Toddler

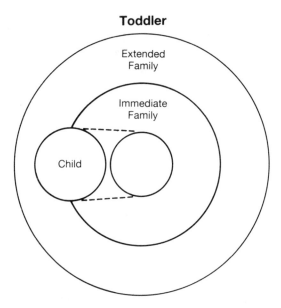

Babies who are abused or who are in a violent home atmosphere exhibit characteristic adjustment behaviors very early. Abused babies may be "flinchy," less prone to seek eye contact. They may avoid smiling, laughing, reaching out, or doing other things that may draw attention. On the other hand, babies in loving homes will smile early, react with pleasure when a parent appears, laugh, gurgle, and show little fear of other adults.

The foundation stone of a lifetime, the self-image, is already being laid at this early stage.

The Toddler

Some time before actually "toddling" the child's world expands to include awareness of people just beyond the immediate family. (See diagram above.) Often these people are part of the child's extended family, the grandparents, aunts, uncles, and cousins. This part of their world may also include close friends of the family.

The Toddlers' Job

The main tasks of the toddler are to learn to think and to do. The main activity of toddlers is exploring the world through their senses.

How can you help them do this job?

Will you love them when they are active *and* when they are quiet?

Will you let them start to become separate from you?

Will you let them experiment?

Will you let them keep trying until they learn to do things for themselves?

Will you let them be angry?

Will you set limits of acceptable behavior, then let them test these limits?

Will you let them discover that there are consequences to testing the limits?

Will you let them test the limits of your patience?

Will you let them learn to ask for help and expect to get it?

Will you let them begin to interact with, and imitate, others?

In the mobility of the twentieth century, grandparents, aunts, uncles, and cousins are increasingly likely to be separated geographically. Interaction with these relatives is often too rare for real relationships to be formed. Some children simply never come to know their grandparents or other extended family members.

Special efforts on the part of everyone to travel frequently is important if the child's view of the"world" is going to include these people and the values they represent. As the child grows older, overnight and longer visits with these relatives can also help in this development. It is important to back up the parental example in the child's "world" with others who support parental values.

Sometimes there are substitutes for the extended family in the life of the toddler, such as close friends of the parent. The child will begin to be aware of and in contact with these persons but will nevertheless remain very close to the family. As shown in the diagram the child remains in the center of the immediate family, constantly returning to this point of social origin.

Usually, the examples shown by these relatives are similar to those of the parents. Still, their ways of behaving and speaking, and the values they reflect, are never quite the same as those found in the parental home.

Sometimes, indeed, they may be very different. Parents need to consider this when deciding how much time the child will spend outside the home, and with whom. Parents reserve the right to discuss with grandparents and others specific examples they would rather not have set for their children when visiting.

APPLYING THE PLEDGE

Encouraging children to crawl, stand, toddle, form words—when, but not before, they are ready—is to expect their best. Having your children with you at the table, in the living room, in the car, on errands, visiting friends is to begin to share your life fully with them. Set an example of patience, free expression, and acceptance. Be vulnerable with them. Let them see that you, as well as they, may

Ages 2-6

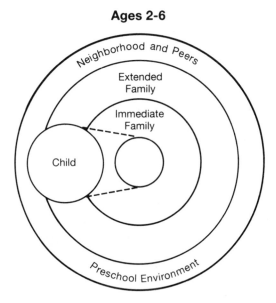

BUSY!

When toddlers are eighteen months old, they really begin to get busy! Here is a parent's log of the activities of one eighteen-month-old for *one* day.

In one day, Mike:

Kicked the springs loose from his bed.

Disassembled his sister's dollhouse and furniture.

Turned over his sister's play stove and sink, removing all the contents, then climbed on it and into it.

Removed the contents from his sister's dresser and record rack, climbed up on a chair and put several records on the record player.

Climbed into his bed, but could not get out again; later did the same thing and fell trying to climb out.

Shut himself in a small space in a closet where the movie screen fell on him and his mother had a hard time finding him to rescue him.

Removed all the books from his parents' headboard shelf, and his mother's jewelry from the box on the dresser.

Plugged in the vaporizer.

Disassembled the night-light.

Turned on the television and "adjusted" it by turning all the knobs.

Removed all the cushions from the living room furniture.

Removed the flowers from the vase and poured out the water.

Poured out his milk three times.

Took the potty chair into the living room, disassembled it, and wore the potty on his head for a hat.

Climbed into the fireplace and played with the tools.

Removed various dishes from the kitchen.

Removed the dirt from the pot containing the Ming Tree, twice.

Removed his new shoes and buried one in the bottom of the toy chest.

Was caught in the act of climbing on a kitchen stool and trying to reach the candy dish.

Shut Speedy (the dog) in the bathroom; climbed on Speedy's back; pulled Speedy's tail; shared his sandwich with Speedy.

Put cereal in his hair; ate two cereal flakes found on the floor.

Scattered the recipe cards around the house.

Climbed on the desk and played with the pencils and address book.

Ate purple chalk.

Removed several light plug safety covers.

Opened and began removing the contents of the drawer in the sewing desk.

feel tired, cranky, or angry without being a "bad," unacceptable person. Discover the things they like to do, the delightful early budding of their strengths, and build on them.

Early Childhood: Ages Two to Six

Children about two to six years old discover that there are lots of "others" out there. Their "world" expands considerably. They begin to move among new people on their own volition. (See diagram, p. 77.)

The job of preschoolers is to establish who they are. One of the ways they do this is through building a network of their own social relationships. They develop imagination, and can create elaborate "play worlds" either on their own or along with play groups. One of their needs is to learn to separate the "pretend" from the "real," and to enjoy both.

While infants and toddlers are taken out by others into contact with other children and families, young children actively seek contact with others on their own. They will want to play with other children in the neighborhood. They may show a desire to visit at the house of a friend, go to a party, or go to the preschool to be with the other children.

APPLYING THE PLEDGE

Young children are ready to tell and expect to be told the truth. Lying by parents at this point creates a lasting gap of trust. Children can now begin to look to tomorrow and plan ahead to develop the beginnings of vision. They can learn that some actions are not acceptable; in learning this it must be clear that a wrong act does not mean they are "wrong" as a person. Share with your children that even though you dislike some of their behaviors, you still love them. Let your own errors be known, and vulnerably accept that some of what you do is foolish. To be vulnerable before a child is to be human, and human is the best example and the best expectation you can ever lead them to.

Children at this age can begin to learn: "There is Someone bigger than even your parent, eternal, loving you, and expecting the best from everyone."

Power, Playing, and Pretending

What is it like for children who have no sense of some power over their life?

Is playing just for fun?

Is "just for fun" a waste of time?

What if a child never learns to pretend?

While the strongest influence on the child remains the parent and home, other values and ways of behaving are learned by the child in play with other children. This does not mean that they should be isolated from the world; that would be impossible, and harmful if it were possible. Children who gain clear examples at home will evaluate their experiences on the outside in terms of the "truth" they see at home.

Late Childhood and Preteens: Ages 7-13

The world of the older child expands rapidly to include a greater number of peers, a large school environment, an expanded neighborhood, and a beginning awareness of the world beyond these. (See diagram.)

A lot of time and energy is spent by preteens in environments outside of the home, and some very close relationships form there. These friendships and the values learned in them will often last a lifetime. Peers and adult friends at this time are very important.

Preteens develop a growing desire to "belong" to a social group outside the family. These are called "peer relationships." When the bonds within the family are weak, and the preteen's need for identity and example are not sufficiently met at home, peer relationships may become the central influence in the child's life.

A balance needs to be struck between home and the outside world. Even when the immediate family relationship is quite healthy, children need the chance to develop an identity that is partly independent of the family. Such terms as: "sixth grader," "seventh grader," "Scout," "Little Leaguer," or "Crip" become important labels acquired outside the family. ("Crip" is the name of an illegal gang of the type found in many areas.) Labels are often applied to the child by others, and by the

Ages 7-13

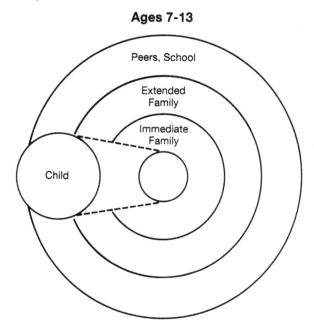

children to themselves to enhance their feeling of identity. With these come the characteristic behaviors, and the values guiding those behaviors, associated with each of those groups. The expectations and identifiers for the male-female roles also develop strongly at this time.

Ties to home become more tentative as dependency decreases, but the preteen still returns to the family unit daily. If home is the place where needs are being met, the preteen still tends to weigh experiences mostly in terms of home-centered values. Comparisons are constantly being made in the child's mind between what is seen to be true at home and in the outside world. While an increasing part of the child's life is happening outside the home, the family still tends to retain the greatest influence.

Healthy interaction and honest communication between parent and child is vital during the child's comparisons of the values seen operating at home with those observed elsewhere.

Preteens are able to begin to tie together the past, present, and future. They can begin to develop a sense of future and can make plans for their life in that future. They can begin to learn the lessons of their own past and that of the family and to learn that there are lessons from the past of humanity in general.

Learning by mistakes is a lifetime occupation. Failure is not terminal. Ridicule is a very painful and very real part of the preteen's life, but it can be survived.

Many parents of preteens, in order to enhance their child's "popularity," may fall into the trap of allowing the lowest standards applied by parents of the child's friends to become the measure of action at home. Tough-minded parents relate experiences to their family's values in a healthy, productive, and understandable way. "We are not guided by the neighbors. We expect, reward, and exemplify and follow the highest vision and values."

Life is a lot of fun. "You are filled with strengths, and each day we will discover more."

"Share with me what's on your mind, and I will listen and hear you; ask me for guidance on what to do, and I will provide it and ask you to do it; share your heart with me, and I will share all the good and bad in truth and honesty with you."

There is a past, a present, and a future. There was a yesterday, and it was important, but it is beyond our changing; there will be a tomorrow, and it will be important, too, and we can impact it! Meanwhile, today is here to be relished.

Adolescence: Ages 14-18

Adolescents move rapidly, and on a daily basis, in and out of all the "worlds" surrounding them up to that time. Shattering the previous personal boundaries, the adolescent becomes increasingly involved in the adult world. (See illustration).

Adolescence: Voluntary Compliance

Physically, adolescents are men and women.

In the past, people often entered the working world by the age of sixteen. After all, nature has us pretty well ready to go by then. In today's world, however, adolescents are physically men and women,

Adolescence
Ages 14-18

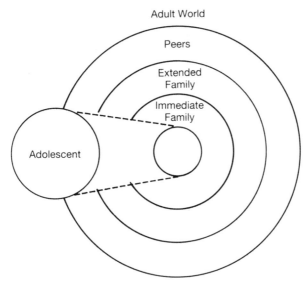

but in a society that is more complicated than they can possibly learn to deal with by the age of sixteen. There is simply too much they need to learn. Because of this, the young person's dependency is artificially continued into the late teens or early twenties.

Young people continue to need the security and support of the family. This need may be easily accepted by parents and teens, or it may be resented. Communication becomes ever more crucial for a healthy relationship.

All of an older adolescent's associations and relationships, including those maintained with their parents, are voluntary. By the time a person is fifteen years of age, and often before, it is well within that person's power to choose, and to take, many constructive or destructive courses of action.

Teens in healthy circumstances will desire and seek guidance, security, and even a certain measure of control from the more mature adults in their lives. They voluntarily follow people they have come to respect.

The mistakes parents can make and more or less get by with at earlier ages become impossible to live with now. A permissive approach can

---

Rehabilitation

If a positive foundation of values is not developed by the teen years, the task is much more difficult but not impossible. Such efforts to correct or make up for what should have been done before are labelled "rehabilitation" or "remediation."

School failure, running away, leaning on drugs, sexual promiscuity, making suicidal gestures, and committing crimes are some of the overt symptoms of the lack of a positive value system. Counselors, remedial schools, therapists, social workers, probation officers, hospitals—all are dealing with these symptoms. While effective work can often be done, it is very hard to reverse the effects of events that are far in the past. They are already moving swiftly in the wrong direction, and diverting them to a new path requires a lot of energy.

How do these situations come about? How do teens, and even pre-teens, get into such destructive patterns? The teens in these situations have often lived in circumstances that are just the opposite of those in a home guided by the pledge of the tough-minded parent.

Their lives might be described more like this:

The worst has been expected from them.

No one has shared or shown love, laughter, and life.

"Faith," "Vision," and "values" have no meaning.

Having been lied to, they lie to others and to themselves.

Examples have been found where ever they could find them.

They have been excluded from their parents' lives.

They have been shown examples of hardness, not vulnerability, and fearful meanness, not tough-mindedness.

The focus has been on weaknesses.

They have been told loudly and commanded: no one has heard them.

They have been led to believe in false outcomes for invalid performance.

The adolescent can sometimes be induced to work on the symptoms, and eventually even on the causes, but unless they voluntarily choose to do this all rehabilitation efforts fail.

How much better it is to do it right the first time!

---

now lead to events that are dangerous not only to the teen but to everyone in the family and perhaps, as with driving a car while intoxicated or without good judgment, dangerous to the rest of the world as well. On the other hand, authoritarianism becomes physically impossible to enforce.

"Rules" are followed by young adults because the values on which they are based have become a part of them. By this time, their values should have created the ability for them to make healthy choices in life.

While interacting mostly with the adult world, the adolescent "remembers" examples set or described at home. A connection remains. The adolescent still returns home, usually on a daily basis, but there is an increasing awareness of the approaching time when they will leave for good. There is a strong and clear awareness of asking for advice, not waiting for directions. Communication, example, and trust become more important than ever before.

For Family Discussion

Have you heard statements like these?
"She's just got to go out and find herself."
"Hey, Man, I'm, like, trying to find myself, you know?"
What does "find yourself" mean?
Where is this "self" that one is going out to "find"?
Is it "hidden" somewhere out in the world?
Does someone else have your "self," and are out there somewhere waiting to give it to you if only you can find them and ask them for it?
If you have a "self" already, do you need to go out and try to find one?
Is a "self" a thing that is to be found or made?
Is a "self" something you have, or something you are?
What if you are unsatisfied with your "self"?

Adolescence: Becoming

"Let each become all that he was created capable of being." Thomas Carlyle, *Critical and Miscellaneous Essays*, 1827

APPLYING THE PLEDGE

All of life, from the moment of birth, is a process of *becoming*. In the teen years we begin to understand the importance of taking responsibility for becoming one's own person.

While teens *can* understand that becoming is a lifetime adventure, they do not automatically learn it or accept it. As with the acquiring of values, a sense of becoming is best learned by example within the family.

Where will this example come from? Are you, as the parent, a person who is becoming?

Are you a parent who sets an example of growing, seeking, delighting in discovering both the new and the old, acquiring new skills, and willingly risking failure?

As a parent, can you expect the best from yourself? Can you enjoy watching your children learn to do the same?

As healthy teenage questioning leads to doubts and wanderings to paths you might not prefer they try, can you lead them to know that you will always accept and love them even if you dislike what they do?

There is a time for every purpose under heaven.

Your children are moving through the world of values that you make available. They are doing that now. They will only pass that way once.

They are growing in your light.

What kind of experience will it be for them?

6

Disruptions and Handicaps in Values Development

"Which of you, if his son asks for bread, will give him a stone? Or if he asks for a fish, will give him a snake? (Matt. 7:9-10, NIV).

Many children have a very hard time growing up. We have seen that the "world" of growing children expands as they move through time. The illustrations we have used would work best under fairly ideal conditions. In the real world, however, we know that such is often not the case. Life sometimes deals parents—and children—some pretty hard knocks so that they find themselves under very adverse circumstances. Some of these are events over which we have little control—but many are within our power either to prevent or to modify.

The first thing we need to do is try to understand. What happens when the situations are not so ideal? How are values to be learned in some of the more complicated circumstances parents and children often must live with in the real world? Let's look at some examples.

The Immediate Family In Conflict

Parents are individuals. Marriage partners sometimes discover that they have dissimilar or even conflicting values. At times one or both parent may even have a serious problem, such as an addiction or an abusive or violent tendency. A child in such a situation is often torn between two sets of expectations. Young children believe their parents are omnipotent, incapable of being wrong. When children find that the two supposedly omnipotent people in their life do not agree in their omnipotence, their world becomes very confusing. (See diagram, p. 88.)

Young children realize their total dependency. They have, therefore, a great fear of losing one or both parents and will often seek ways to

Immediate Family in Conflict

please them both. In the conflict situation, pleasing them both is impossible, and the attempt is highly stressful.

Children in such circumstances find no consistent values and no standard whereby to select one set of values or the other. In fact, these children have motivation *not* to select one set of values to avoid offending, and perhaps losing, one or the other of the parents. They may then develop no real values at all.

On the other hand, such children may resolve the conflict by overtly choosing one parent over the other, thus fueling the conflict in the family by having "taken sides." Often, they change choices from parent to parent and back again.

It is vital that parents who have trouble avoiding conflict do their best to try to resolve their differences. At the least, they must realize the effects of their conflict on their children and spend some time in unity with their children as the focus.

Children from such homes need help to be aware of the effect these conflicts have on them, to understand that they are not to blame for

their parents' inability to communicate or resolve conflict. They also
need help in developing their own value system.

The Child of Split Parents

Many courts now engage in the practice of awarding "joint custody"
of the children to divorcing parents. In such cases, and even in cases
where there is a clear designation of the legal custody being with one
parent, the child is "split" between two households. The child travels
physically from one household to another, often on a weekly basis. Numerous problems stemming from inconsistent value orientation arise
in such cases. (See illustration.)

All of the who, what, when, where, how, and why questions are
answered differently in each household. Therefore, reality is defined
differently and calls for an adjustment in lifestyle with each change in
temporary residence.

The physical surroundings are different. Children derive security
and part of their identity from the house and the variety of items in the

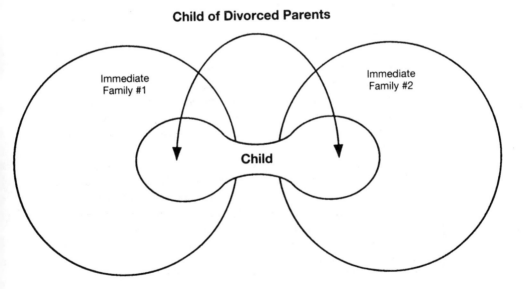

Child of Divorced Parents

Immediate Family #1

Immediate Family #2

Child

house. A child may have a room designated as "your room" in each house, complete with furniture, decorations, and even separate clothing wardrobes. All of these physical things that help to support a child's unfolding identity are different in each household.

The expectations are different; word usage is different; discipline is different; the rationales as to why things are done in certain ways vary; the neighborhoods and peer cultures are often different. In one home, the child may be seen as a welcome member of the family. In the other, the child may be a reminder of an unpleasant past or perceived as a threat by a new spouse.

Most importantly, the values are different. No two households will hold identical values. In most instances, we expect children to be exposed to different values in different households as they move about through the extended family or peer culture. They can handle this if

---

A WOUND NEVER HEALED

Children of divorce are often in an information vacuum, with no control over events that profoundly affect them. They often feel that it is their duty to try to solve the parental problems, that it is somehow their fault. They are often in conflict over which parent deserves their loyalty, worried about where they will live, fearful that their parents may harm each other, or even that they may be harmed.

Divorced parents, and those who work with their children, must understand a basic truth about virtually all divorce situations where there are children: In the child's heart, the desire to see the parents together again will never go away. This is true no matter how well the children rationally understand the permanency of the split, how fully the child accepts the reasons for it, or how much time goes by. It is true even when the divorce brings relief to a painful situation for them.

Emotions are not rational; they are very powerful; and they are timeless. Children will act on their emotions when no rational basis exists for them to do so. They may say or do things that they wish might result in a reconciliation, including misbehaving. They strive to hide from unpleasant truth, and to believe that the world can magically be made over. The same qualities of the heart that are the wonderful core of childhood are the most vulnerable to distortion.

they have a consistent "home value base" to return to. In the split family, the child has two homes, and, inevitably, two "home value bases," adding to the confusion.

Parents in these situations must do their best to talk together about the children without regard to fixing blame or "scoring points" in their marital or divorce conflict. They need to share accounts of the children's lives. They must agree on basic expectations, standards, and discipline. A consistent parental values-formation plan must be agreed upon, coordinated, and maintained.

Each parent is still a parent.

Televison: The Anti-Vision Medium

Children are constantly being removed from their home values as effectively as though they were taken for several months of every year to another world. Few parents would knowingly choose this world of negative values. We are often so careful about the day care, the pre-school, the friends, and other examples of our children will see. Why,

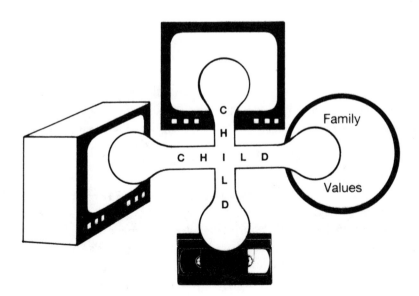

then do we turn them over to the passive television babysitter who fills their minds with uselessness and harmful examples of how to live? (See diagram, p. 91.)

It is possible, though rare, to have a house and a life in America today without a television set. There are some families who have made a deliberate decision not to have one. The children in these families never know about the Saturday morning "cartoons." They never see the "soaps." They never sit in their house and see people being killed or beaten up. They never see casual sex on the screen. Of course, they also miss the truly good educational programing and fine quality drama that is available on television. But the parents in those homes have made a conscious choice and consider that they have made a good trade. These same parents, though, also spend the time to provide personal educational and recreational experiences for their children.

There are other parents who have a television set but monitor carefully what the children see. They know what their children are doing and watching. They, too, are spending the time it takes to work with their children. They may select from among the many good video cassettes available for children—select, that is, after watching them first and knowing what they are choosing.

Millions of parents are concerned over what entertainment television is bringing into their homes. Defenders of the television medium challenge their critics to prove that television is harmful to kids. And they have a point. Studies have provided indications that there may be a connection between television violence and violent behavior in children, or television watching and lower school achievement, or television watching and premature sexual activity. But there is always room for scientific doubt. A solid, hard-to-refute, cause-and-effect connection may well be beyond the kind of scientific proof that everyone will accept.

So, if science fails us, what do we use as our guide? Let's try common sense reasoning.

If we tell children that hitting is not a good thing to do, then surround them with examples of people who are constantly hitting each other, what will be learned?

If we tell children that what is on television is unimportant and not to pay attention to it but we sit in fascination absorbing every word and scene, what can we expect them to believe?

Is it truly a pure coincidence that television violence and real violence have increased together?

Is it truly a coincidence that as time spent by children watching television has gone up, school achievement and physical fitness have gone down?

For Family Discussion
Watching Television—The Perfect "Pass" Time

Clay lies still, but blood's a rover;
  Breath's a ware that will not keep.
Up, lad: when the journey's over
  There'll be time enough to sleep.
        Alfred Housman, 1896

Other than sleeping, is there anything that passes the time without action, effort, or thought more totally than watching television? In fact, even sleeping is not time wasted. The body and brain need sleep and use that time very well.

Once a day is gone, isn't it gone for good? How do you retrieve an hour gone by? We don't advocate constant productivity. Rest and relaxation, of course, are good for everyone. But can't we find something better for our time than watching television?

Consider the entertainment value of:
  Talking.
  Listening.
  Taking a walk.
  Playing a game.
  Reading a biography.
  Studying your religion.
  Reading to your children.
  Learning to play a new sport.
  Practicing sports you already like.
  Learning to build a piece of furniture.
  Coaching your child and your child's friends.
  Helping your child learn how to make something.

Let's think through Housman's poem:

"Clay lies still"

Clay is dead. It is inert. It does nothing and knows nothing. It is passive.

"Blood's a rover"

"Blood" means life, and life's a rover. It moves. It has volition. It sees, hears, learns, and is aware. It is active.

"Breath's a ware"

A "ware" is a thing of value. Life has value. It is of limited supply.

"that will not keep."

Life is of limited duration. It does not store well. Life is a perishable ware.

"Up lad."

Be up and into life. Live it, don't watch it.

"When the journey's over"

Every journey has an end. So does the journey of life. While you're on the road, see, hear, take part in, interact with the whole scene—now, while you can.

"There'll be time enough for sleep."

Death is the ultimate passivity. Why get started with it any sooner than necessary?

Are you just passing the time?

Do you want your children just passing the time?

How can you help them become motivated into activity?

Will your life, and theirs, be spent in passive staring?

We hope you will talk about this as a family.

In this book, we have urged families and individuals to develop vision. Vision is a very active process. Vision involves seeing yourself and others doing something and being something in the future. If one is not actively doing and being anything now, how can one envision doing and being anything in the future?

We develop vision by living, acting, and becoming. Watching television is the exact opposite of acting and becoming. It suffocates vision. Entertainment television is an "anti-vision" medium. It is purely passive—more passive than sleep—almost as passive as death. Passivity is the enemy of creativity, thought, life and vision.

For Family Discussion
Prime Time Television—Clear and Present Danger

Have you really thought about the ultimate results of television role models? Their appearance is haphazard or narcisistic. Their language and grammar is third-rate. Their persona tends to be shallow, downbeat, and flippant, with terse, thoughtless answers for everyone. Listen to the one-liners by adults and children in some of the "sit-coms," then you be the judge.

How concerned are you about what's happening to our young people? Are you willing to continue to go along with the sheeplike acceptance of popular stereotypes such as: "Television programming only responds to the desires of the people." "We give them what they want."

We believe deeply that the rising tide of addiction, suicide, streetkids, and all the other signs of trouble cannot be solved by excellent parenting alone. We parents must also have the guts to say to television programers, "Enough." Television must be dramatically overhauled, cleaned up, and led by tough-minded parents.

The strident and virtually sick crescendo of violence, sex, and perversion on prime time television is a national disgrace. As long as we, the parents permit it, indeed *support* it, why should our kids believe in our credibility?

This indictment in no way refers to such fine programs as *Mr. Rogers, Sesame Street*, and other good children's shows, although, many of the products advertized on some Saturday morning children's shows are questionable. We mean, *prime time television*!

Since our *value* is the sum of our *values*; since minds are the products of what they ingest: since our children ultimately become what they see and say, how can we possibly condone a steady diet of such phrases as: "So help me, I'll kill ya!" "You're dead meat!" "We blew him away." "You want me, I want you, so what's to lose?" America leads the world in violence and television watching.

You are challenged to start right where you are right now. Write to the networks, call them, meet with parents groups in your community who have the courage to act. Fingerpointing and denunciation won't do it. Tough-minded parental action is needed!

Yet, we seem to think of television as "a necessity." What is a "necessity"? There are many modern necessities that we surely want to keep: indoor plumbing, electric lights, water heaters, automatic furnaces, laundry machines. All of these, although our predecessors once made do without them, are genuine necessities of modern family life. If we had to do without them, we would be giving up an important part of the quality of modern family life. They enhance our health. They allow us to do other things of real value. They give us time that we can use to spend with each other, if we will.

Or, we can spend that time watching television.

A television set is considered to be one of the basic necessities of a modern household. We often even have special rooms for television, ironically called "family rooms." How necessary is it? Would you like to try the following exercise?

For a month, keep a log of how much time each person spends watching entertainment television. Exclude genuine educational programing. At the end of the month, put your television set in a closet and leave it there for a month. Keep a log of how each person spends the time they would have spent in front of the television. Compare these logs. Discuss the comparison as a family.

How much money could you get from selling your television set? Enough to buy real assets, like books, hobby equipment, games, bicycles, hiking shoes? Or maybe even just a lot of pizza to eat while the family has conversation.

Regain your vision! Take control! Care enough!

The Bread or the Stone

Children are a gift to us, and a wonderful opportunity for the shaping of life. They ask of us the gift of life, a life worth living. Would we starve them? Or would we give them bread? Would we experience the tremendous joy of seeing our children grow through a happy childhood into fine adults? Or would we suffer to watch them struggle in pain and die?

They ask for bread.

"Which of you, if his son asks for bread will give him a stone? Or if he asks for a fish, will give him a snake?" (Matt. 7:9-10, NIV).

"Things that cause people to sin are bound to come, but woe to that person through whom they come. It would be better for him to be thrown into the sea with a millstone tied around his neck than for him to cause one of these little ones to sin" (Luke 17:1-2, NIV).

What will we give them?

7

Your Child's Expanding World of Values

"Jesus grew in wisdom and stature, and in favor with God and men" (Luke 2:52, NIV).

What is REAL Growth?

One of the central themes of this book is that the best measure of growth for children, and the greatest contributor to growth by other measures, is the strength of the value system which guides them through life.

We can place the finest nutrition before our children in the most delicious form imaginable; we can provide excellent classrooms and cleverly presented training in academic and problem solving skills. We can provide services to care for the emotional trauma that children may experience. Yet far too many of our young people do not take advantage of what is offered.

By contrast, there have been many situations in the world in which nutritious food has been genuinely scarce, text books outdated or nonexistent, school rooms unheated, teachers untrained, and yet children have developed amazing intellectual capability and growth in skills.

So, what determines whether a child will grow? Is there a factor beyond the quality of the food or the physical and educational facilities? Yes! A young person selects a good diet because a healthy body is valued. A young person learns academics because of the value that is placed on learning. A young person strives to excel in sports, drama, art, or in social skills because of the value on that endeavor. A young person feels free to express emotions honestly because of the self-assurance that a firm values system bestows.

98

Growth has four dimensions: physical, mental, emotional, and spiritual.

A strong values system is a reflection of spiritual growth. It is the determiner of whether a child wants to grow in the other ways we so often concern ourselves with: physical, mental, and emotional.

The Laws of Child Development

We believe:

Children grow only when they want to.

Children who want to grow will, regardless of inhibiting circumstances.

Children who are equipped with a positive value system will want to grow.

On of the Beatitudes says it well: "Blessed are they who hunger and thirst for righteousness, for they will be filled" (Matt. 5:6, NIV).

Our goal as parents and as a society needs to be to create and nurture within each of our children a thirst for growth. This thirst will come only from within, from the faith, vision, and values of the young person. Children who think of themselves as worthwhile people will want to grow and work to grow.

For the purposes of this book, *child development* is defined as: the growth of the child's value system and self-worth. (See diagram, p. 100).

Growing children gain values from the world they experience. For children in a healthy, growing situation, that world expands as the years go by. First they are aware of their parents and of the immediate family. Then they become aware of the extended family, the neighborhood and peer groups, the church, school, and community. Finally, they discover the nation and the world at large. For each child, these are the "present" parts of the "world"; these make up the world that is now, represented in our diagram above the lifeline.

Values, however, are not gained only from our present world. There is also a world of the past. Growing awareness of values for children also involves a growing awareness of the roots of our values in past human experience, represented below the lifeline. Understanding the role of the past in values development increases the validity children see in those values.

Beyond these, the child's self-image is also based on a perception of self as a part of the future. In our diagram, we show the growing young

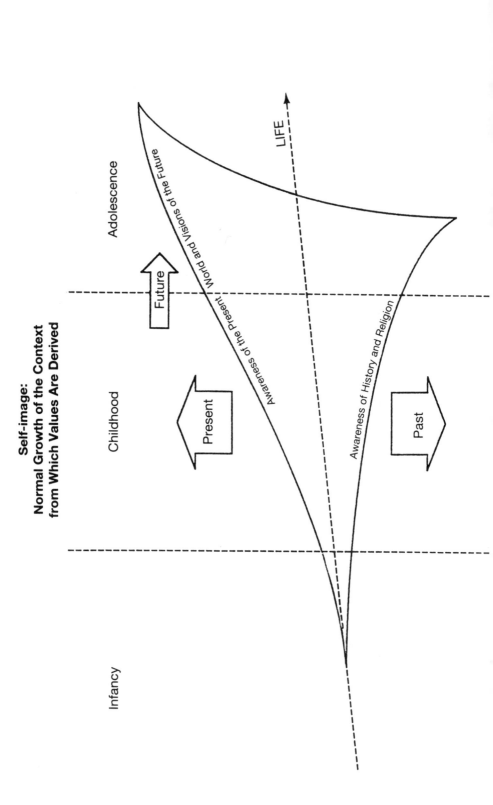

Self-image:
Normal Growth of the Context
from Which Values Are Derived

Infancy

Childhood

Adolescence

Future

Present

Past

World and Visions of the Future

Awareness of the Present

Awareness of History and Religion

LIFE

person's awareness of self in the present social world as reaching forward as a surging, reaching wave, anticipating and eagerly stretching to embrace the future.

For Family Discussion

1. What does it mean for a person to learn more about:
The world of the present?
Where the world of the present came from?
What has been written and said in the past?
What humans have come to believe to be true because of a history of reaching for religious understanding?
What has proven to be worth living for over the great stretch of human experience?
What may come to be in the future?
2. How can you feel more important, rather than less, by learning how truly big and old the world is?
3. The future is unknown: how is it frightening or exciting?

The Development of Vision

Our tough-minded view places great importance on the strength of the self-image. Self-image has a future dimension; it doesn't only exist "right now." We see people as growing, developing, stretching, and seeking. Part of the future aspect of the self-image is simply a growing awareness:

- that there is a future;
- that we can imagine ourselves in that future;
- that planning for the future is exciting and important; and
- that it is desirable to dream.

This awareness of the future is essential to human life and is a vital ingredient in our value system as well. Each person has the choice of "living for the moment" or "living for a better tomorrow," and to one extent or another we all make that choice every day. Shall we spend every dollar today or save at least a little? Will we think in July about a warm coat for December? Is there something at home for dinner to-night, or tomorrow, or next Tuesday? What do I do to prepare for the examination next week?

Teaching our children to realize that tomorrow is real, that they will be in that tomorrow, and that it is necessary to prepare for tomorrow are among the most basic goals of child development.

Ordinary human living is impossible without at least a rudimentary future awareness enabling us to deal with the future—to see what is *possible* and be ready for it. Therefore, future awareness is the view of the possible.

Is a rudimentary future awareness enough? Is that all we want? No! Our diagram intends to convey a much more dynamic concept: that of the person's ideas reaching forward as a surging, reaching wave, antici-pating and eagerly stretching to embrace the future.

This is the development of vision. Vision is the transcendent view of the possible.

To transcend means to go beyond thinking about what has always been believed possible and to believe that there is nothing that is impossible.

Using figure 12, we have been describing the growth of the self-image and the development of our view of what we *are* in the world. This growth is not, however, merely a matter of gaining more of the same as time goes by. It is not simply expanding our horizons outward in the world, backward through time, and forward through time. At some point in the growth and development illustrated in figure 12, truly growing people begin to acquire the quality of vision. These peo-ple have not merely practical view of the possibilities of the future and their place in it, but a truly transcendent view of those possibilities—fueled by hope.

Vision is that quality which allows us to look beyond what we are today to what we can *become*. It is a view of a world that, through our efforts, may also *become more than it is today*. It is the discovery of our possibilities and a thirst to realize them. It is a desire not only to move ahead with the future and be a little bit ahead of your time, but a thirst to reach forward as a surging, reaching wave that races toward the furthest, most challenging horizon, eager to see not what is on that horizon, but beyond it. This desire is fueled by hope.

Ad Astra Per Aspera
[To the Stars Through Hardships]

Parent, what is your vision for yourself? Your family? Your world?

What values do you have that will aid your family in realizing your vision?

Do you hunger and thirst for justice, knowledge, righteousness, abundance, and honesty for yourself, your children, and the world? What example do you provide?

Would you like to surge forward eagerly into the unknown? What steps can you take right now to begin?

Do you look for the possibilities in yourself, your family, and those around you?

Will you help your child realize the truth of the Latin proverb, "Ad astra per aspera" [To the stars through hardship], by daring to reach for the stars yourself and to welcome the hardships along the way?

Parents who wish to see their children fully and truly develop will earnestly desire for their children to acquire *vision*.

It is elementary that leading by example, serving as the role model that we want our children to imitate, is the most effective way to bring about a desired result in anyone else. All of the best teachers, managers, leaders, evangelists, and parents know this truth. If you want your child to develop beyond the mere practicality of future awareness to the development of vision, the best way is to exercise vision within your own life.

For a continuous increase in the strength of our physical, mental, emotional, and spiritual muscles we must keep stretching forward and using those muscles, fueled and pulled by hope.

On the Shoulders of Giants

There are many experiences parents hold in common; those kinds of events that, when talked about among parents, cause heads to nod and smiles or frowns to appear as the listeners remember going through the same happenings with their own children. One of these is placing your child on your shoulders so he can see over the heads of a crowd, or to touch the ceiling, or to carry him because he is tired, or merely for the fun of it!

This is a simple illustration of a basic truth: the higher you are to begin with, the farther you can see and reach. If children are to attain a state of continuous growth and forward reaching, they need to have the deepest and highest foundation they can find. If the foundation is there, all that is required is for the child to climb up on it. Parents can help in this climbing process, but only by climbing with their children all the way! This foundation, illustrated on page 100, is past human experience, religion, and history. People follow a learner, not a knower.

We thought it would be more than appropriate to turn to our panel of experts from the past to find some helpful ways to illustrate and communicate this concept.

Robert Louis Stevenson wrote many lovely poems for children; his work reflects a high degree of empathy with the childlike mind of unfettered imagination, and they are recommended reading for all parents and children. He wrote of his shadow, playing imaginary games on the bedcovers when ill, and one of his best: "Foreign Lands," which we can remember hearing read as children until it became memorized.

Foreign Lands
1881

Up into the cherry tree
Who should climb but little me?
I held the trunk with both my hands
And looked abroad to foreign lands.

I saw the next-door garden lie,
Adorned with flowers, before my eye,
And many pleasant places more
That I had never seen before.

I saw the dimpling river pass
And be the sky's blue looking-glass;
The dusty roads go up and down
With people tramping into town.

If I could find a higher tree
Farther and farther I should see,
To where the grown-up river slips
Into the sea among the ships

To where the roads on either hand
Lead onward into fairyland,
Where all the children dine at five,
And all the playthings come alive.

What a picture of a child reaching and climbing and developing *vision*! He was helped to do so by gaining height and increased perspective through his own endeavors. How much richer the world is because of the adventurous, stretching mind of Robert Louis Stevenson. May we speculate that Stevenson had the encouragement of tough-minded parents? Is it a coincidence that his father and grandfather were famous engineers and builders of lighthouses?

Sir Isaac Newton, who made world-shaking advances in the human understanding of how the universe works, humbly reminded others of the fact that he had the help of many who had gone before: "If I have seen further. . . it is by standing upon the shoulders of Giants."

Foundation

The past provides a great wealth of moral thinking, practical thinking, and examples. In the past we find the great religious revelations that represent our attempts to understand our spiritual nature, the nature of the Creator, and our ultimate destiny. No moral choice your child will ever face is new in the world. A great many ordinary and extraordinary people have been faced with them before, and their success or failure is recorded in writing or in lore. Their stories and their words are available to us all.

Newton was not speaking to parents (so far as we know!) when he proposed his Laws of Motion. In considering the proper encouragement of a child in healthy directions, however, a parent might well benefit from thinking about these laws.

Every body continues in its state of rest, or of uniform motion in a right line, unless it is compelled to change that state by forces impressed upon it.
The change of motion is proportional to the motive force impressed.

People differ from inanimate objects in one way because they are moved by example and encouragement better than by force. Still, without some kind of outside motivation from the significant people in our lives, most of us might have remained "at rest." Further, children often need to be shown the direction in which they ought to be moving, particularly when on a collision course that they might not see unaided.
Newton might also be remembered, when considering leadership. He described how the heavier the body is and the nearer it is the greater effect it will have on those around it. If you want your child to follow your lead, to move in your orbit, the best way is to carry the greatest moral weight around and to keep a close relationship.

Children who grow in knowledge of the past, and who continue that pattern throughout life, have a huge advantage over those who do not.

Children who know the biographies of the great strivers of the past have unmatchable role models to help them as they encounter the painful and difficult problems of their own lives.

Children who study the Scriptures of their faith are in touch with the truth and are building a foundation of values that will never fail them.

Child development is incomplete without an expanding awareness of past human experience.

The oldest member of our panel of experts reached into the past of his time for wisdom that is as valuable to today's parents as it must have been to those in Egypt 4,400 years ago:

"Teach him what has been said in the past; then he will set a good example to the children of the magistrates, and judgment and all exac-

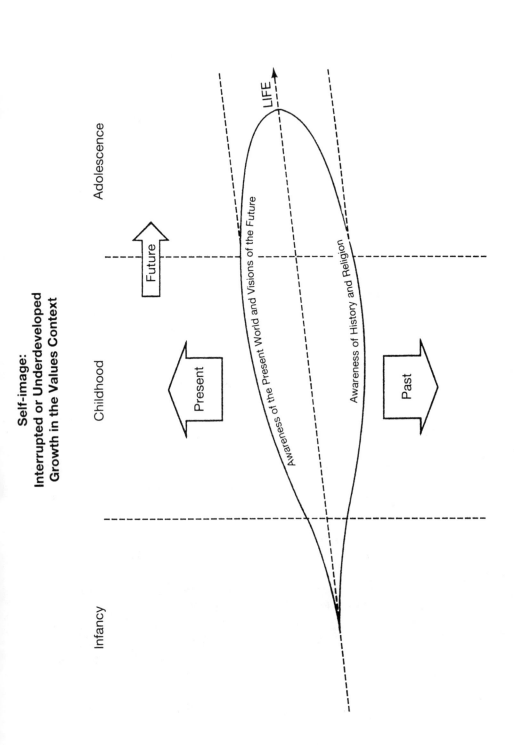

Self-image:
Interrupted or Underdeveloped
Growth in the Values Context

Infancy   Childhood   Adolescence

Present

Future

Past

LIFE

Awareness of the Present World and Visions of the Future

Awareness of History and Religion

titude shall enter into him. Speak to him, for there is none born wise."
—*The Maxims of Ptahhotpe 24th century B.C.*

How many parents would have been spared terrible anguish over their children if only they practiced that last line of wisdom! If we could shout into the ear of every parent every time they looked with horror at something their child has done, it might be the words of Ptahhotpe: "Speak to your child! Speak to him, for there is none born wise."

Translated into the terms of tough-minded parenting, this maxim becomes: "Share wisdom with your child and listen so that you may both become wiser."

Toward the Void: The Incredible Shrinking Child

It is clear that we are seeing in our society an alarming number of young persons whose value development is dangerously inadequate.

All children, early in life, experience some growth in their understanding of the social world around them. If they did not, they would remain emotionally crib-bound. They learn about, and move within, an expanding world of family, neighborhood, school, and some of the world beyond. They learn some history in school; some learn a little about the past from parents, extended family, and friends; those who attend a church school are exposed to enough basic concepts of religion to least know that some people believe there is a spiritual dimension to life.

The development of a value system begins at birth. All too often, however, there is such an anemic example to follow that value development stops. The need to grow and learn does not stop. Often, however, at about the beginning of adolescence, the desire to grow and learn will begin to wither if there is no parental example to lead it. Understanding is like a living thing: it is either growing or it is dying. Without growth the adolescent's knowledge of the present, the past, and the future wanes and dies.

Without a world of values, the child will develop a void in place of a self image. Without values, they will place no value in themselves.

People of any age who cease to expand their horizons of awareness will begin to see those horizons shrink. Their present, past, and future perspectives contract. Like the brightness dying in a light bulb fila-

---

Act Out—Drop Out

Without a solid and growing system of values for guidance, and without a vision as a reason to exist, hopeless, self-destructive behavior is inevitable. Such a young person is easily turned aside into such behavior as use of drugs; promiscuous sex as a substitute for love, acceptance, and achievement; suicide; criminal behavior; rejection of family, friends, church, and community.

---

ment when the current maintaining it is cut off, the vision slowly dies.

As vision dies, the values already in the early stages of development lose meaning and the temptation to compromise one's standards increases. A narrow view and compromised standards leads to a narrow

---

For Family Discussion

Another sad reaction to a weakly developed value system may be a sort of withdrawal into "dead-end" behavior. With only fear and without hope, some people fall into a nonchallenging daily routine pattern that is simply intended to maintain life, nothing more. Examples are:

Fair school attendance, but with no effort beyond the very minimum required to stay out of trouble;

Jobs without a future, minimally performed, day after day, year after year;

Relationships with no challenge, no growth, no struggle;

Complacency;

Complete lack of interest or involvement in hobbies, civic events, and issues, voting, church, or learning anything.

Is this "get-by" pattern familiar to you?

We are all aware of the more visible young people engaging in destructive actions like drugs, suicide, or crime that draw our attention, but doesn't the "dead-end" represent an equal failure?

Where does this "slouch-out" behavior lead?

How would it feel to be in a cycle of "dead-end" behavior?

How can it be changed?

Is this passivity dehumanizing?

What does it mean to be a "human being" to you and your family?

---

view of the self. The self-image zeros out. A person who has no stimulus to grow begins to deteriorate quickly to a void, and the self begins to disappear.

Rights

At the center of any value system is the matter of rights. One of the most profound statements of the values central to our society is our Bill of Rights. This set of amendments to the Constitution defines what the unchanging legal rights of an individual are in relation to the evolving power of the government. The rights held by each person help to form a secure basis for a strong self-image. Individual rights are a part of the firm foundation of the past, a guide to the present, and our hope for the future.

This is also true of the family. At the center of all evolving family relationships is the vital matter of rights. The values-centered and value-led approaches we advocate throughout this book require a clear understanding of the rights we all have. Here are some of the rights all family members have, and some they do not have.

We each have the right to:

1. Feel our own feelings.
2. Choose how we will think and act with our feelings.
3. Learn from our mistakes.
4. Ask questions.
5. Meet our needs, remembering that others also have needs.
6. Change our behavior.
7. Be true to ourselves.
8. Say no responsibly.
9. Believe in God.
10. Have our individuality.
11. Choose laughter, joy, and success.
12. Recognize our strengths and use them in our life.
13. Have and express our own opinion.
14. Fail.
15. Dream.

Steven's Rights: (Contributed by Steven, son of one of the authors, age six).

1. Ask for help.
2. Be curious.
3. Learn.
4. Sometimes have things our own way.
5. Love ourselves.
6. Be loved.

We do not have the right to:

1. Judge others.
2. Place demands on others.
3. Expect more of someone than is agreed upon or than they can reasonably give.
4. Expect others to accept responsibility for our actions.
5. Live our lives through our children or others.
6. Live our children's lives for them.
7. Destroy our bodies with chemicals.
8. Deliberately hurt another person.

To be appreciated, rights must not only be recognized by others but *asserted by the individual.* Children need to assert their rights in a healthy way that also respects the rights of others. If parental power is used to override the healthy rights of children, how will they develop the strength to assert themselves in the outside world? If they cannot assert themselves when they need to, what will become of them?

No Middle Ground

Child development is: the growth of the child's value system and perceived self-worth.

There are two choices for the development of the self-image: growth or gradual death.

Our values are the core of our being. They condition all that we say, do, and are.

Will your children grow in understanding of the present, past, and future world? Will your children acquire a constantly stronger base of values for guidance and success? Will your children surge forward into the future on an exciting wave of hope and vision?

Will your children learn to value themselves and develop hope?

Do you care enough about the future of your family to place the pursuit, acquisition, and practice of excellence in values at the top of your priorities?

8

Whose Child Is This?

Children spend a lot of time with people other than their parents. Children develop within many environments beyond the immediate family and are profoundly shaped by each of them. This chapter discusses the important environments in our society which influence children and the ways the children are affected by them.

Child of the Extended Family

The family is the center of the child's life. Often, the term "family" is used to refer only to those who live in a single household. We might say, for instance, "The Clark family lives two houses down from us." When talking about a certain child, "family" usually means the child, parents, and any sister or brothers. But there is a "family" that extends beyond these, called the "extended" family, made up of others related by blood or adoption. Grandparents, aunts, uncles and cousins make up the extended family.

Grandparents in particular can be very important to children. They often are the first stimulus to the building of a values foundation beyond the parents and beyond the present into the past. Many of us have the pleasure of seeing our children mature and relating to them as adults. Many of us will have the pleasure of seeing our children have children of their own.

What does it mean to be a grandparent? Your child is grown, and the job is done, right? Wrong! There is no point in our lives when we can "shut off" or "cut back on" love, concern, and supportiveness. If your child is grown and you have just discovered some things you wish you had known and done when they were younger, it is not too late to act.

113

Growth and improvement can be accomplished at virtually any age. We are never too old to change and grow.

One of the authors tells about such a situation.

"Some years ago I was working as a consultant to the chairman of the board of a large company. The chairman offered me the presidency of the company at a magnificent salary. This truly astonished me because he already had a son in the business who possessed exceptional academic credentials and was only one year younger than I.

"Why not promote Sid to the job?" I asked.

The answer was a grim, set facial expression and a flat, emotionless voice. 'He's never really had anything on the ball. I'm disappointed in him. He just doesn't have any of my qualities—he'd just foul this company up, I'm sure.' The chairman proceeded literally to detail the weaknesses he perceived in his son. It was a painful litany of hopelessness.

"I declined to take the position of president and asked Jim if I could do an in-depth assessment of Sid. I spent many hours with him and then set up an all-day meeting with both father and son at a remote and private meeting room.

"Early that day, we began an all-out search for, and exploration of, the strengths of each of them. Weaknesses were clearly defined as only missing strengths or as insufficiently developed strengths. Our focus on strengths became sharpened and intensified as the hours passed. First, each man was asked to write down twenty strengths he perceived in himself. This was tough for them, because each had built his life around the stale and stereotyped notion that a preoccupation with weaknesses could accomplish positive things.

"When this exercise was completed, each was asked in turn to take plenty of time and share out loud all the strengths he could perceive in the other.

"It is a fundamental truth that we only see and relate to the strengths and possibilities of others when we can perceive and relate to our own strengths. Sid and his father each had a knee-jerk tendency to lapse into pointing out the weaknesses of the other or to make light of their own strengths.

"Initially, there was some profanity and flushed and awkward expressions. Bit by bit each was helped to see that the reality of the other was his present and potential strengths. By the end of the day, they embraced—and tears flowed. Release and catharsis was under way!

"Additional strength focusing sessions were held—always in private and carefully monitored by me. Sid was promoted to president, and Jim planned to retire in a few years.

"Six years later, Jim was sixty-eight. He was suffering from cancer and knew he would not live much longer. I'll remember his words all my life. 'I can't tell you how pleased I am with the way Sid is doing. The company is prospering as never before and—much more importantly—the time my wife and I spend with Sid's family is just great. The grandchildren and I have more fun that I ever believed possible.'"

Please don't assume from the foregoing that everything was smooth and simple. There were many rocks and shoals; however, the focus on strengths was the linchpin for the application of tough-minded values, insights, and techniques. It required determination, tenacity, and courage. It worked!

John Greenleaf Whittier said,

> For of all sad words of tongue or pen,
> The saddest are these: "It might have been!"

A very well-known and wealthy man who had spent the bulk of his career as a successful politician said, "The one major regret in my life is that I was so busy campaigning for office and doing all sorts of important things politically that my two daughters grew up and I never really got to know them." As he said this, his eyes moistened and his voice trembled. I thought of the following poem.

> My hands were busy thru the day...
> I didn't have much time to play
> The little games you asked me to...
> I didn't have much time for you.
>
> I'd wash your clothes, I'd sew and cook,
> But when you'd bring your picture book
> And ask me to share your fun...
> I'd say "a little later, Son"

But life is short, and years rush past
And little boys grow up (real) fast . . .
No longer is he at your side
His precious secrets to confide.

The picture books were put away
There aren't any games to play . . .
No good night kiss, no prayers to hear . . .
That all belongs to yesteryear.

My hands once busy now lie still;
The days are long and hard to fill.
Gee, I wish I might go back and do . . .
The little things you asked me to.

Tough-minded parents or grandparents take time out to feel love and gratitude for family, and to risk sharing them with others.

There's Still Time

"I realized with real shock that I've been expecting my kids to fall short in about everything I've asked them to do. I've been cynical and sarcastic and reminded them constantly of what a perfect guy I was when I was their age. I've compared them unfavorably with me. And, you guessed it, they deliver what I expect. There may still be time to be a really good parent yet."

And there was.

Does this sound familiar? This was a comment of a member of the Baseball Hall of Fame, who is now in public relations. From time to time since then, he has updated me on their family's progress. The boys are now grown men, and he says that he and his wife feel very good about what has happened.

We become what we think, we become what we say. Above all, we become what we expect or believe.

Child of the Court

Many children today have some of their most important life-shaping experiences in the court system.

The court system is one of the major institutions of our time, and we are all profoundly affected by it. Every society creates a system to resolve question of truth. In the Western world, and especially in the United States, the court is our final source of truth when we cannot agree among ourselves. We turn to the courts for our answers to land disputes, personal squabbles, failed relationships, and questions of guilt and punishment. Some of these disputes involve children.

In most ways the courts of the Western world serve their purpose well. The guarantees of fairness and standards of proof that have evolved over centuries of legal experience usually assure that injustice against the individual is as unlikely as possible. While truth often remains elusive, at least there is a real attempt to be fair in arriving at decisions. All parties usually have a chance to "state their case."

There is a real price to be paid for this due process of law, however, and that price is time. The demands of fairness require time to prepare your case, time to be notified of the case against you, time to assemble witnesses in your behalf. The courts, therefore, move slowly. The problem with children in the court system is that the courts move on "adult time" and children move on "children's time."

Einstein told us something about time that we already knew. Time does not always pass at the same rate. Any five-year-old will tell you how very long the time is before the birthday party and how short the time is during the party. Time is indeed relative. It is relative to how much time one has already lived. Time is, therefore, relative to age— the perception of time's passage depends on how old you happen to be.

Children in court are the victims of a terribly destructive time warp. Due process takes time, and that's something that children just don't have a lot of. As decisions are made in a divorce case, a child abuse case, or a delinquency offense charge, the child involved continues to speed along at the "child rate" while the court drags along at the "adult rate." As the time used up for court procedures creeps by, the child races through a large portion of a total lifetime of experiences, and is continually changing. By the time the case is decided, the child is in many ways a different person than when it began.

What happens to the quest for the truth—concerning the child? The child and the child's world have changed significantly while the court was seeking an answer. "Truth" to the child has changed faster than the process can discover it.

For Family Discussion
Whose Baby?

Several years ago, a juvenile court case in a major city involving the custody of an infant became so complicated with conflicting claims of parents, grandparents, the state, and social agencies that there were eventually five lawyers arguing for the various points of view. This went on for weeks, both in and out of the courtroom. Meanwhile, the infant was in foster care in blissful ignorance. This poem came out of the juvenile court staff office:

Baby McGee

"Whose baby? Whose baby?" the lawyers all cried.
"How in the world will we ever decide?"
"My client's child!" "No! Mine!" the retort.
"Indeed," said the Judge, "He belongs to the Court."

A quintet of lawyers. No two could agree
On who was the owner of Baby McGee.
Meanwhile, will McGee just sit on a shelf?
Poor child. He thinks he belongs to himself.

There are three types of cases involving children in court.

Divorce

Nearly half of all children in the United States will experience a divorce. In most of these cases, parents manage to decide who will have the custody of the children without a contested court battle. When the parents cannot decide, however, the courts decide for them, often after lengthy "due process of law" and bitter adversarial struggle. Each parent strives to win the contest, citing and often exaggerating every blemish in the life of the other parent. In the course of the court battle, one parent is often proven to be less fit, or somehow worse, than the parent who wins custody. To some extent at least one, and sometimes both, parents are "destroyed" in the eyes of the children.

Child Abuse

Hundreds of thousands of children are brought to the court for custody decisions due to physical, sexual, or emotional abuse by parents who are supposed to be their protectors and mentors. Parents have a right to be presumed innocent, and accusations of abuse must be proven by due process. These decisions take time, and the children are often placed in temporary care for many months while the "truth" is being discovered. Some of these children may never return to their natural parents. Some may be adopted. Other may be raised in foster care by people who cannot possibly provide total healing to a traumatized child.

Juvenile Crime

Still another group of young people, usually adolescents, come before the court for having committed crimes, or delinquent acts. These children find, due to their own behavior, that their parents have been forced to turn decision making over to the court system. The parent is not the major figure in this situation. A young person accused of a crime has the same rights as an adult charged with a crime, and his lawyer is his best friend. The lawyer's job in the criminal case is to require the state to prove the case, which often means to allow the accused to evade the truth unless it can be absolutely proven.

All of these court experiences—divorce, child abuse, juvenile crime—have the following points in common as seen by the children involved:

1. Children of the court see that the family as a social institution does not work to solve the problems in their lives.
2. Children of the court see that the court works so slowly that its answers are irrelevant from their perspective.
3. Children of the court see that when accused of wrongdoing, the truth is relative to what can be proved.

"Dying with Their Rights On"

Rather than seeing the best example, children of the court are shown the lowest standard of values available, (that which can be proven).

1. Children feel that they are of secondary importance. All other matters come first. The child's home and care are only determined after all of the important matters of property and law are taken care of.

2. Children feel unprotected. Children don't understand legal proof. They don't know that if acts harmful to them cannot be proved, they didn't happen. They don't know that if an act cannot be proven to be harmful, it wasn't—no matter how much they know they have been hurt.

3. Children conclude that values are meaningless as guides to their behavior. They can see that the line is not drawn on their own harmful behavior until they have had every opportunity to evade responsibility. They can see that the system encourages them to do exactly that.

Children of the court operate at a severe handicap in the race for the full development of a value system which can guide them to success. They are far more likely to reach the point of zero growth and begin instead to die. A juvenile court judge in Iowa said in 1979: "The kids are dying with their rights on."

It is the *children's* experiences in court that shape them, not the adult-oriented court records. We must try to see what the court experience looks like from the child's point of view.

The Child of the School

A central theme of this book is the crucial importance of excellent expectations. Schools are a very important environment, impacting the growth of children. What role do expectations play in the achievement of students in our schools?

School achievement varies greatly across the nation. Every year, schools in Iowa, North Dakota, Nebraska, and some other states report the highest achievement measures in the nation. Students in Germany, Japan, Sweden, and certain other countries also exceed average American achievement. What is the secret of the consistent educational achievement of these states and nations?

It isn't money. The top-achieving states in the United States typically spend less per pupil on education than the national average. Nor are teacher's salaries in these states especially high. Facilities and equipment are pretty good but no better than a lot of other states.

The "rural-urban" differences don't account for the differences in achievement. These differences seem to hold when the comparison is with other largely rural states as well as with large metropolitan areas. Also, some of the nations with higher achievement are more urbanized than the United States.

What accounts for superior school achievement?

The best place to look for the answer may be in the values prevailing in the populations. The high-achieving states and nations remain comparatively family centered, and cohesive families most often have a tradition of expecting the best from each other and delivering it. These same families also expect the best from their teachers and administration and encourage their schools to expect the best from their children.

The real determinant of educational excellence is found in the home, not in the school.

Advance Through Achievement—or the Passage of Time

What are we expecting of our children? Are we, perhaps, getting just what we expect?

One of the issues that continually arises in schools is whether children should be retained in a grade if they fail to meet the learning expectations of that grade—the minimum requirements for promotion. This used to be called "flunking a grade."

Children think of themselves in terms of what they hear. They tend to believe what powerful adults say about them. They tend to believe that they are what we say they are.

An important part of a child's identity has to do with how they perceive their advance through the stages of childhood. It is very important, for example, to become a "first grader," or a "bluebird," or "Webelos," or a "confirmed member" in a religion. The child's self-concept changes as this advancement occurs. The child will tell you "I am in first grade," or "I am seven years old," or "I am a Scout, now, not a Cub."

These achievements usually result either from achievement, having completed a prescribed series of activities in an acceptable manner; or from the passage of time, merely having become a year older.

Scouting offers an example of advancement that depends upon achievement. Kids move through the ranks of Tenderfoot, Second Class, and so on to Eagle by virtue of having learned and demonstrated certain oaths, laws, skills, and other indications of serious intent that can be evaluated in fairly clear terms. Adults tell the children whether they have made these advances. As they achieve these advances, their self-concepts develop accordingly.

On the other hand, schools often offer an example of advancement that depends mostly on the passage of time. In many instances, children will be advanced through the grades whether or not they have learned the skills and concepts that each grade is supposed to impart. Hence, a child is an eighth grader principally by virtue of being fourteen years of age.

This type of advancement has an impact on the self-concept. A certain amount of perceived increase in status goes with advancement through the grades. With each passing year, children feel that the status that goes with being in whatever grade belongs to them simply by virtue of their being there. And why shouldn't they believe this? After all, the adults promoted them to that status, so it must be true.

"If you hold back the child for lack of achievement, the child will be out of place with the younger kids. He will have social adjustment problems. He will think there's something *wrong* with him." This argument is heard repeatedly from the education establishment when merit promotion is urged. And it's partially true—as far as it goes. The child who is not advanced a grade will certainly feel out of place, but he will know the reason why. That child will, in fact, be in the place that has been earned, and so will those others who met the expectations that went with their advancement.

Children will respond to expectations. What can parents do?

Flunked Through School

What happens when we advance children regardless of achievement?

What happens when we simply promote students through the grades as a reward for having lived the required number of years?

What happens when these students reach adulthood?

When these new adults graduate, but cannot read, cannot balance a checkbook, cannot make change, cannot mark a ballot, and cannot earn beyond minimum wage, will they not then truly feel out of place?

At that point, will there not truly be something wrong with them?

What about their self-esteem when they are unable to find meaningful work?

What about the potential that went unused because we were afraid to expect the child to develop?

People who graduate from high school without basic skills are often very angry; they have a right to be. We have failed them by allowing them to fail themselves. We have truly "flunked" these children out of school with a worthless diploma.

Child of God

Whatever humble place I might hold,
Or lonely trails I have trod,
There's a child who places his faith in me—
There's a dog who thinks I'm God.
Lord keep me worthy, keep me clean
And Fearless and Unbeguiled—
Lest I lose caste in the sight of the dog,
And the wide, clear eyes of the child—
Lest there come in the years to be
The blight of withering grief—
And a little dog mourns for a fallen God,
And a child for a lost belief.
—Author Unknown

One of the most awesome responsibilities and most wonderful privileges is the leadership role we have as parents. By our actions, reactions, words, and body language, our children can see us as people to love and value; or they can see us as people to escape from. We can build value into our children, or we can create in them feelings of failure and of being valueless.

The importance of a role model in every young life is crucial, yet all of us are human and sometimes do things wrong. Parents don't always know the direction they ought to be going or where they ought to be leading their children. How can we be as certain as possible that our direction is right?

Here we can turn to the Pledge of the Tough-Minded Parent in a different way and at the same time turn to our spiritual faith. When you, as a parent, need direction, ask, listen, and hear at the level of the spirit. You might get off by yourself and simply say, either aloud or just within your mind, "God, I don't know what to do. Help me."

"What then," asks the skeptical, technology-age parent. "Will I hear a voice? Will there be a sign? Should I expect a burning bush?"

No. The answers don't come in twenty-second sound bites complete with audio-visual effects. We must ask with our whole person, listen the same way, and be willing to hear the answer. As we review the record of human interaction with God, we find few instances when specific and detailed directions are given. The answer will most likely not come in the form of what to do, but what to be.

We do not expect intimate, effective interaction with a person whom we do not know. Why expect it with God, unless we know Him? It takes time to build a close friendship, or a marriage, or even a good working partnership. Start working on your relationship with God now.

Children must build their connection with God on their own. Parents cannot do this for their children, but they provide a role model.

When we learned to ask God "What do you want me to be?" we are on the way to receiving answers to the questions, "What should I do with my life?" and "How can I most help my children?" Asking what we ought to *be* is the most-fundamental, most-important step in our life as a unique human beings, in our life as a child of God.

How we feel, what we think, and the choices we make based on these thoughts and feelings, write our own destiny. When we know

---

For Family Discussion
"I Am"

Everyone gets to decide whether or not to look at themselves as being connected in some way with God. There are many ways to practice being a child of God, but the first question always must be: "Am I a child of God?"

Is this a question you want an answer to? Why or why not?

Where can you get help in answering this question?

Do you know someone who believes they know the answer? How can you tell if they really do?

How would I hope my child would answer this question?

---

who we need to be, we will find it relatively easy to know what to do. Who is guiding us on our quest as parents and as growing individuals? Are we children of God? Has God given us our children? Can we stop and ask and listen for the answer? We can choose to be grateful for our children and the privilege of their love and the opportunity to guide them, or we can choose to resent all of the time and energy they take.

You might begin by simply asking yourself and God, "What do you want me to do with my life? What do you want me to be?" The next question is, of course, "How will I know when I have an answer? If there isn't going to be a lightning flash or a written guarantee, how will I know if I have an answer I can trust myself and my children to?" Listen. When you are listening, be ready for the probability that the answer you get will not be easy. It may be downright tough! If an easy answer comes to mind, chances are that it's not the one your looking for. The answers to the difficult questions are as difficult as the questions. Be ready to express gratitude for the challenges you may be faced with.

We ask, and we want to be given an answer. Are there ways to recognize a gift of an answer? What gifts have you already been given? Chose first to be grateful for yourself and for your children. When you look at your children, do you really see them? their strengths? their feelings? Do you find something to be grateful for about them nearly every day?

Do you see your son or daughter with love and laughter and gratitude? Or, do you see them as the reason you are so tired, the reason you have a headache?

Ask—Listen—Hear

To learn to recognize an answer as a gift from God, learn to recognize the gifts already received. It then becomes easier to ask for guidance and to listen and really hear the answer from God and from our children. The more we live gratefully, the more vulnerable and sensitive to our children we can be; the more we really can hear what they are saying.

One happy father as he talked with us about his children and his life, said: "When I was growing up, I was told and thought I understood, that if you see yourself as a unique and potentially splendid creation of a loving God, you become potentially splendid. Quite a wonderful way to see ourselves, isn't it? But if you see yourself as a second-rate loser, you will become, in effect, a second-rate person! So I told myself I was full of strengths, full of potential; but I never asked God whom He wanted me to become. I thanked Him for my splendid potential and went right ahead and did what I wanted to do. I thought splendid thoughts and tried to be the person I wanted to become.

"It didn't work because I didn't listen to my own feelings—to my heart. I listened only intellectually, and I tuned out God. My mind was managing my decisions, not my spirit or my feelings.

"Today I know how I feel and I know who I am, but tonight I will ask God to share with me His will for my life. I hope once more that I will listen and hear. As a father, I will also ask for guidance for my daughter and my son. They, too, are splendid, but my hope is that they can learn the power in this philosophy: The more I ask, the more I give. The more I listen, the more I hear. The more I have each day to be grateful for, the fear of feeling, of being vulnerable to life and fear of taking risks fades. When I choose to truly feel grateful, my heart opens and I can *hear*."

The Church

It is important for the parent to find as many reinforcements for their values in their child's world as they can. Consistency in example and teaching strengthens the developing value system. The church offers a unique opportunity for growth in all dimensions to children and adults.

1. It expands the child's awareness of the *present world* by adding a place that is consistent with what the family believes.

2. It builds the child's awareness of the world of the past and the way those values were successfully followed then.

3. It has a vision of a future and helps the child to look forward with hope and expectation.

4. It provides role models, information, and encouragement for the development of a personal faith.

Choosing the right church for your family is only the first step. You may discover that any church you choose is not quite what you'd like it to be. How can you see to it that you have the kind of church environment you want for your child? Make it happen! Your church, your neigh-

---

"Let Them Decide"

"I'm not going to make my kids go to church. I'll wait until they're old enough to understand, then let them decide."

How many times we have heard this! "Let them decide." We do advocate letting children decide as many things as possible. We also recognize that, in the long run, children will decide the important things for themselves, such as whether to go to church and which one. But what goes into that decision? What do children use as a basis for deciding?

1. Example. Children do what we do, not what we say.

2. Experience. children can make better choices acting on a basis of experience than without it. Are they more likely to choose something they are familiar with and that has been rewarding, or something they know nothing of at all?

3 Values. If you feel that the values of your church, or of a church you can find, are what you want your child to acquire, then what is your choice? If you can't find a church that has values you consider to be positive, ask why not. Maybe you expected to find perfect people there. Where else have you found perfection? Expect the best—that's all you can do with a church, a child, or yourself.

borhood, your schools—all are dependent on people to be the best that they can be. Become involved; serve on committees, attend the services and the church government meetings. Become informed, then let your opinions be known, then help to make things happen.

Practical Attitudes

Do you ever feel bitter or depressed? We all have these feelings sometimes. That's a human trait, but it's one that we have the power to change. Can you think clearly and productively in a bitter and depressed frame of mind?

Now think of the times you have felt thankful. Is there a difference in your overall attitude?

It's so easy to get caught up in despair and frustration and begin to wallow and focus on bitterness and the things we resent in ourselves, our children, and our life. It is easier at these times to see what is wrong rather than what is right, what is good, and what we have to be grateful for! But the choice here is ours alone to make. We can remain stuck where we are, or, with God's help, we can choose to change our rigid attitude. We can choose to take responsible choices and grow.

"I just have so much pain!" a young woman said. "I can't deal with the stress of living much longer. I am really glad I am not a parent, because I can't cope with myself right now. If I had a child, I know I would abuse it. I would lash out in anger, because I can't even deal with myself right now. How could I cope with someone else? I counsel parents all the time about child abuse, but I can understand how it happens. I can look back now at my own parents and see their unhappiness. I can see why they seemed so unloving, so resentful of me. But what could they have done to change? What can *I* do to change?

This young lady gets to the heart of many of the parenting problems today. For those of us who grew up feeling unloved, alone, a child of no one, it is virtually impossible for us to feel free to love our own children and our spouse. So what can we do? We can make a conscious choice to decide to change; decide to do some serious thinking and feeling. Take time out for yourself and plan to spend one or two hours in a quiet place. List those things for which you feel grateful. List reasons you are grateful to your spouse, yourself, your son, your daughter.

After listing your gratitudes, begin a list of all the strengths you have. If you get a little struck on that one, go back to the gratitudes and analyze why you are grateful. For every every gratitude you have, you should see a strength in yourself to also be thankful for. Only after we know what our strengths and abilities are and ask how we should use them can we make decisions about where we want to go with our lives—who and what we should be. We trap ourselves with our attitudes and we trap our children by them.

Extreme rigidity or extreme permissiveness are hard attitudes to live with. Tough-minded attitudes result in tough-minded parenting. A rigid parent might try to tell the child how to think and what to do but be unwilling to listen to the thoughts and feelings of the child. A permissive parent gives in to the child's every wish even when the parent and the child both know it is wrong. A tough-minded parent works with the child to develop clear behavior guidelines and asks, listens, and hears what the child has to say. We have the right and the power to make decisions based upon our personal value system. But only by using our strengths as the basis for our decisions can our actions be productive and lead to the fulfillment of personal and professional goals. When we as parents know who we are and what our values are, we can teach our children values.

The quality of our inner life can lead to abundance in every way. What you feel is who are you. It shapes and affects all that we say and all that we do and especially the way we affect our children.

As we can accept our strengths and gratitudes and teach the process to our children, we can learn to value each other and God. Learning to feel, to let ourselves open up and surrender to what God asks of us is the beginning of faith. Without faith, life becomes a meaningless scramble, a meaningless series of attempts to give yourself the physical and material comforts of life. Faith, hope, and love are the real vitamins of the person. Add gratitude and it fuses these into a unified whole.

Gratitude and depression cannot coexist! Where there is gratitude, there is hope. Where there is hope, there is purpose and direction. Fuel this hope with faith and love and you have a person who knows *who* they are, *where* they are going, and *why* they want to get there!

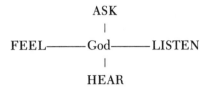

We can only teach our children the value of this if we identify with it ourselves. We must become as a little child.

Let the Fun and Renewal Begin

In Romans 12:2 Paul says, "Be transformed by the renewing of your mind" (NIV). But as we renew our minds, our spirits must be let loose. Be free to grow, free to feel. One of the great traumas in many lives is learning that intellect cannot heal. Our minds can think all of the right things, while our body and spirit are dying. To be well, emotionally, spiritually, physically, and intellectually is to be open and vulnerable and to begin to let our spirits soar.

One beautiful example of this is the story told by Norman Cousins in his book *Anatomy of an Illness*. This internationally known intellectual shares the story of how, when traditional medical treatment was failing and he seemed to be dying, he determined to get well through a nutritional and positive-thinking approach. He contrived all sorts of experiences and experiments that would make him *laugh*. Yes, *laugh*! There is a healing quality in laughter that no chemical medicine or drug can duplicate. He began his "get-well" process by using his mind—and we *need* our minds—but the healing actually began when the laughter filled him.

We are not talking about tense, strident laughter wrenched out of people by cynical, sarcastic, caustic, or weakness-oriented "humor." Rather we are talking about laughter that wells up inside of us because we can *feel*! Some of you reading this today have been lucky enough to have had a parent or grandparent who loved life and laughter. What a wonderful example!

One of the biggest impediments to the popular acceptance of the "wisdom" of many wise people down through the ages is that they have tended to utter those profundities in austere, severe, tight-lipped, *humorless* ways. They appeared to be intellectual, but very unfeeling. What child will want to take a risk, work hard, do something tough if they see us, their parents, as unhappy and dismal over our own risks? Of course, one cannot accurately predict the outcome of any situation or control what will happen, but who even wants to start if they expect the end result to be gloomy?

Laughter is truly one of the most undervalued elements of life. *Think* humor and laughter. *Feel* humor and laughter, and above all, let it *out*. Psychological research has clearly indicated the almost total *absence* of humor in the mentally disturbed and ill. Such research has also clearly established laughter as an essential emotional nutrient in high levels of "wellness."

To live with renewal and evergrowing feelings of significance, look for reasons to laugh and *share* laughter.

So, enjoy yourself! The Bible says, "God loveth a cheerful giver." (2 Cor. 9:7, KJV). In the original Greek this phrase says, "The Lord loves a *hilarious* giver." How about that? Have a *hilarious* time. It's *good*, it's *right*, it's *moral*, it's *healthy*!

G.K. Chesterton, in his great book, *Orthodoxy* said, "There was one thing that was too great for God to show us when he walked upon our earth; and I have sometimes fancied that it was His mirth."

9

Some Nuts and Bolts of Tough-Minded Parenting

We strongly believe that there are certain fundamental truths about parenting; we also recognize that we are in a world of change. What seems permanent, stable, and reassuring today may be unrecognizable or gone tomorrow. Our children face a world that is in many ways unfamiliar to us, and that can be frightening when we try to prepare them for a tomorrow that can't really be imagined. Helping them learn to be strong, resilient, and flexible has never been more important.

Like sailors near a rocky and unfamiliar coast, we seek for beacons, compasses, and sextants to help us find our way. Our children might use the modern-life analogy of an airplane pilot needing directional radio beams to aid in instrument flying in foggy weather or an astronaut needing accurate gravitation maps for precision landing on the moon or Mars!

In this world of continual change, specific guidelines and imperatives for parents are needed as never before. We offer you some beacons, directional beams, and gravitational maps for successful parenting today and tomorrow.

Twenty-one Recommendations for Successful Parenting

1. The tough-minded parent provides an example that is positive, stretching, loving, and healing.

A fine example is worth 10,000 words. We all lead or parent by example, even though the example is sometimes not what we intended it to be. The key question concerns whether it is the right example—the best example we can provide. Is your vocabulary, tone of voice, body language communicating what you want to communicate? an example that is worthwhile, striving, stretching, reaching, and changing? It requires *growth*.

The story is told of a child who was caught stealing pencils at school. His father was dumbfounded. "I don't know why he needs to steal pencils. Don't I bring plenty of them home from the office?"

We have, over a period of twenty-five years, interviewed and worked with hundreds of youth brought to juvenile court for theft. One fact is clear about thefts committed by young people: *juvenile theft is almost*

For Family Discussion

What is the focus of activity for your family?
What is the focus for each of you?
What point is made in the following letter?

The Essence of a Good Parent

Dr. Barbara Brock
A "New" Working Mom

A good parent is one who cares enough to spend a few more hours at home and a few less hours at work. Those hours might only be spent, for instance, in various aspects of the "Discovery Principle." In this activity, time is spent discovering multitudes of obvious and hidden things, preferably outside. The discoveries should be divided unequally, with the less-experienced partner finding more than the older one. The only criteria are that the television may not be turned on, the computer must be turned off, and telephone calls returned later.

By leaving work a bit earlier than the norm, this parent may have to postpone a few meetings, reach lower rungs on the ladder, and lose some face in the professional "dog-eat-dog" world for a while. The payoff? A child, bringing many new discoveries, a little bit of eternity, joy in its purest form, a priceless fountain of youth, and the real essence of love into a busy and harried world. This is one parent who may aspire to achieve the best of both worlds as a working mother, but who must strive to be "good" at work and "great" as a mom.

What does this statement mean to you: "Where your treasure is, there your heart will be also"? (Matt. 6:21, NIV).

What do you treasure?

---

never the result of a need for the item stolen. Young people usually steal:

—because of an insufficient inhibition against it;

—because they feel a need for the excitement of the act; or

—because of the extreme importance placed on materialism in the family.

If you cheat on your taxes, steal materials or time from your employer, leave after a minor accident without leaving your name, what do you expect from your child? If you give your child toys instead of time, cash instead of affection, what will your child believe to be important?

If you tell your child only what you think she wants to hear, will your child tell you the truth? Each of us is faced daily with decisions about the truth. In countless ways we set an example of either telling or avoiding the truth.

Each of us is faced daily with choices regarding taking or avoiding responsible action, rising to a challenge or retreating from it, growing or stagnating. These are impossible to hide from children. They watch, they see, they hear, they become what we are.

2. The tough-minded parent asks, listens, and truly hears.

Do your children feel that you are approachable, interested, and concerned? Telling, pushing, threatening, driving, and coercing have not met the test. They have never been validated by positive, responsible, and loving results. Review your methods constantly to help ensure that your children feel you are approachable, nonthreatening, interested, and concerned. Fathers particularly often lose sight of how often they are perceived as threatening.

"I can't say anything without my mom finishing the sentence for me. She always thinks she knows what I'm going to say and even what I'm thinking!" This statement, made in private to one of your authors, followed an interview with a mother and her sixteen year-old daughter that went somewhat like this:

OFFICER TO SAMANTHA: "Samantha, what brings you and your mom to the juvenile court?"

SAMANTHA: "I . . ."

MOTHER: "She doesn't want to go to school, and now she's taking the car and driving while drunk!"

OFFICER TO SAMANTHA: "Ok, let's take one thing at a time, Samantha. What about school?"

MOTHER: "She goes to school only when she feels like it, and that's about once a week."

SAMANTHA: "I go more than that."

OFFICER TO SAMANTHA: "How much school are you missing in an ordinary week?"

MOTHER: "Last week you weren't there at all."

OFFICER TO MOTHER: "I'd really like to know what she has to say. We need to know why there's a problem."

MOTHER: "You can't believe what she does say."

OFFICER TO MOTHER: "What does she say?" (Pause.) "Mrs. Sachs?" (pause.) "What does Samantha say to you about what is happening?"

MOTHER: "She won't tell me anything!"

The problems in this case were not complicated, certainly not as difficult as some others with similar behaviors. What was needed was simply for the girl to be able to share with her mother the ordinary triumphs and difficulties she was experiencing: friends, homework, feelings of attraction to boys and their approaches to her, worries about her appearance and capabilities. Samantha was running scared with no one to talk to. Her school difficulties were merely a symptom of this problem and a plea for attention.

Samantha's mother had her own feelings of doubt and inadequacy, job worries, single-parent budget problems, and working out her own relationships with men. She needed someone to listen to her.

These two needed each other. They needed to share, listen, and, above all, to *hear*.

3. The tough-minded parent leads the family to a clear vision of what the family can become.

Excitement, stimulation, and motivation occurs more effectively in a family where Dad, Mom, and the children all have a feeling that their family is significant, that each of them is significant to the family, and that there is purpose and focus in the overall "grand design." Stretching goals are not only pluses, they are essential for a feeling of unified growth and progress.

"A victory for me was a victory for my parents—for everybody in the family," said a thirty-year-old as he remembered his childhood. "When Mom came home with her college degree, we celebrated. When Judy marched in the band, we all went to watch. When I was promoted to Webelos, everyone was there. (Mom had to be—she was the den leader!) We all got together and set a goal of saving for a trip to Colorado, and everybody worked together on it. We held a family council once a week, where we exchanged good news about ourselves and each other, heard about the family finances and other circumstances, and came to agreement about our plans."

4. The tough-minded parent provides much love and trust, and expects the best, within reason.

If a child receives sufficient and abundant amounts of these three ingredients alone, the deck is truly stacked in favor of positive growth and successful maturation.

"By the time the kegger was over, the house was in pretty bad shape— and so were some of the kids." This statement, from a juvenile court case, had been given by the fourteen-year-old son whose parents had left him in charge of the house for a day and a night. Viewing the scene, I had to agree. Windows had been broken, some rare and expensive glassware had been thrown into the fireplace in which a chair had been broken and burned. In general, the place was a mess.

Along with the property damage, two of the kids had gone to the hospital to have their stomachs pumped when they consumed too much liquor from the parents' liquor cabinet too quickly. One was estimated to have consumed what would have been a lethal dose of alcohol and, if not for timely medical attention, would have died.

There had been over twenty teenagers ages thirteen to sixteen years in the house. All of them had been out with their parents permission. All had been trusted by their parents. Every one of the parents expressed surprise and shock that their trust had been so betrayed.

What went wrong? Don't we preach that parents need to trust their kids so they can learn to exercise good judgment?

Conversations with these parents revealed that they really should not have been so surprised. The party and the deceptions that made it possible were thoroughly planned, well executed, and easy. Each teen simply told his parents that they would be staying overnight with one of the others, and instead they all went to the party. Not one parent verified their child's alleged overnight arrangement. The kids knew they wouldn't, because their parents did not know each other and did not communicate; *none of the parents had ever even spoken to any of the other parents, over the telephone.*

The trust and good expectations were present; however, the expectations had not been backed up by the investment of parental interest, time, and energy—the reflections of love.

Care Enough to Know

Children like to be trusted. They also like to receive high expectations and the attention necessary to see that those expectations will be met.

Children are bright; they know that no one cares about anything they don't take the trouble to know about.

One of the great messages we continually receive from children of all ages is: "Care enough to know about me, about my friends, and about what I am doing." This is a message all parents can well reflect on.

Loving trust does not mean being a patsy or a sucker! Trust cannot stand alone. Love, trust, and expecting the best are inextricably intertwined. Ten-year-olds, for example, are not trusted to drive an automobile, because they are not yet ready to meet that trust. Loving trust means knowing where your children are going to be, who they are going to be with, what they will be doing, and when they will return. Checking to be sure that all the adults supposedly involved know that you know what's going on does not reflect a lack of trust. It reflects loving trust, which conveys the best expectations through being informed and involved.

5. The tough-minded parent believes that the finest gift you can give another person is the gift of an excellent and stretching expectation based on a never-ending search for their present and potential strengths.

When we expect the best from our children, we lead them toward excellence—a term that has been overused and underunderstood for some time. Perfection as a goal sets up a sure collision course with failure! Excellence, defined as "giving a thing your best shot and knowing it," provides a path for growth in skills, understanding, and self-esteem. Such a flexible, stretching concept of excellence recognizes that what may be excellent for one person or one endeavor, may be mediocre for another.

The Family Strength Bank

One of the most productive practices in a tough-minded business enterprise is the establishment of individual and company-wide strength banks. Each team member is encouraged to enter in a notebook each day a newly discovered personal strength. In addition, the company as a whole maintains and updates, often by computer, a list of the perceived strengths of each team member.

This will work for families, too. There are several ways to start and maintain a family strength bank. If you have a family council, you might begin each session with a few minutes in which each person hears compliments from the rest of the family and states what they think is a new strength they have discovered in themselves that week. Each person can maintain an individual notebook listing personal strengths. This notebook should be reviewed from time to time by parents or other family members. This practice can be carried out even if your family doesn't meet in a family council, but it may be more effective with wider participation.

Excellence Defined

Strengths vary from one person to another, and so must expectations. What is consistent in everyone is the ability to do one's best. Excellence consists of the desire and effort to do your best.

What a reward there is in hearing your parent tell you that you have done your best! What gift to your children to expect the best of themselves. What a foundation for confidence they will build by learning how much they are capable of achieving.

Don't worry about some arbitrary, external standard. If your children learn to put forth their best effort every time, they will meet any reasonable standards and *exceed* most of them. If your children learn that competing with yourself brings greater achievement than competing with others, they will find themselves setting the standard that others try to match!

For Family Discussion

Hope

What does the following mean to you?

Expectations are utterly and totally the stuff of hope, and all constructive and healthy plans, actions, and accomplishments are fueled by hope.

What are your dreams? How can the family help you put some real muscle into your dreams?

Do you dare to confront your hopes? How can your family help you realize your hopes?

Do you care enough to ask much from life?

Do you care enough to seek strengths in all things? How will that make a difference?

Do you care enough to replace cynicism with wonder?

Do you care enough to remove the negative, "apostrophe-t" words from your vocabulary? What are some of those words? How will that make a difference? Do you really become what you say?

Do you dare to share the real you with others?

How do you distinguish between "tranquility" and real happiness?

Do you care enough to lead?

---

6. The tough-minded parent believes love is the toughest-minded emotion in the world.

This is a strong statement! Please note the nine ingredients of love as described by the apostle Paul:

Patience . . . . Love suffers long
Kindness . . . . And is kind

Generosity...............Love envies not
Humility ....Love is not proud
Courtesy ....Does not behave itself unseemly; is not rude
Unselfishness ....Is not self-seeking
Good temper............Is not easily provoked
Guilelessness............Takes no account of evil
Sincerity ....Rejoices not in unrighteousness but
                         rejoices in the truth.

Things cannot be great. The only greatness is unselfish love. What we are stretches past what we do. One of the great abiding statements of love is by Christ who said: "Whoever welcomes a little child like this in my name welcomes me" (Matt. 18:5, NIV).

Touch Me—Love Me

Lee Halverson, doctoral candidate at Drake University, Des Moines, Iowa, reports on the importance of touch as his research on the subject unfolds.

"From childhood to adulthood we all need caring, nurturing touch. As babies, our skin is the largest sensory organ of the body. Babies who do not receive caring touch will have difficulty growing into fully functioning adults who are capable of loving others. In the teen years, children deprived of touch will seek it outside the family and in many cases through immature sex. Children provided with touch as they grow need not seek it from those who would hurt them.

"As adults, our marriages stand a much better chance of survival if we keep each other alive by touching. We then feel cared about and belonging, just as our children will in touching homes. Our children need to see our parents model appropriate loving touch.

"The elderly are also wonderful caring touch models for children. Both the elderly and children, when provided the opportunity to come into contact often, gain a great deal, and receive the message that they are valued and belong."

Let us not give in to the fear of caring touch that seems to be descending on us as a result of the genuine concern over child abuse. If we allow ourselves to be frightened into being afraid to give children the appropriate loving touch they crave, we shall have truly lost a generation to them.

7. *The tough-minded parent never makes a decision for a son or daughter whenever the young person is qualified to make that decision alone.*

The "use it or lose it" principle applies: If you do not exercise an ability, it atrophies. Doing something for a person when they can do it for themselves often diminishes rather than enhances their confidence, dignity, and individuality. We learn to make decisions by making them. We learn to make *good* decisions by taking our chances on making mistakes.

The young child is not ready to decide to take a trip across town, or even across the street if there's much traffic. But the young child can decide whether to play in his room or in another room. He is not ready to decide whether the weather requires a coat, but he can decide what color to wear.

The Hollow Oak Tree

"On rainy days, our daughter was given an umbrella to hold while waiting for the school bus out by the road. As she got to be about ten years old, she learned that It wasn't cool to be seen by the other children holding an umbrella. So, when the bus appeared about half a mile away, before anyone could see her, she would fold the umbrella and stick it into the hollow of a tree that stood by the road. By the time the bus arrived, she would be as wet as if she hadn't had an umbrella at all! But, by her decision, the damage done by the rain was more acceptable than being seen with an umbrella. She seldom remembered to pick up the umbrella on the way home. At one time, there were four umbrellas in the hollow of that tree at once."

We want our children to make decisions that make sense, that work in the real world. Some of these lessons can only be learned through trial and error. A child can only really learn about the practical working of the force of gravity by trying to "walk on air" from one piece of furniture to another. They best learn that the dog should be left alone when asleep by poking it and being nipped.

We want our children to make decisions that follow our values. The best guide to our children is the example we provide for them by the decisions we make. Still, the only real route to building their own moral strength is through experience in weighing the moral alternatives and experiencing the results. They make the decisions, and the world, sometimes aided by the parents, provides the lessons.

8. The tough-minded parent recognizes that true commitment to a promise, goal, or project is best facilitated when the young person understands the what, where, when, who, how, and, above all, the why.

This simple-sounding formula has been tested many times by people who want to move beyond mere dialogue and establish true communication. This mental checklist can provide much help in creating a family environment of teamwork and synergy. It works!

"What, where, when, who, how, and why" are the important things to find out about anything. Every little child knows that—and asks incessantly—until we discourage them. Go ahead and answer the child's questions; you'll learn new answers of your own! The tough-minded parent knows that "the truth sets you free," and steadily strives to teach and exemplify this.

Why?

The heart and soul of a person, a family, an organization or a nation is found in the reasons why they do whatever they do. It is the motivation for doing. It is the evaluation of what is done. It is the measure of what is worth doing. It is the essence of being. If you can determine why someone is behaving a certain way, you will know who that person is.

Providing ourselves and our children with good answers to the "whys" will provide a piece of the foundation for happiness. Good reasons "why" will assure that the decisions as to "what" we do, "where" we go, "when" we do anything, "who" we do things with, and "how" we do them will be answered nobly.

---

9. The tough-minded parent is consistent and timely with discipline.

Here, the power and desirability of asking, listening, and *hearing* is manifest. Family guidelines and rules need to be clearly established, mutually understood, and consistent. Prompt, informed *response* is what we're advocating, not uninformed reaction.

Timeliness is extremely important. Basic learning principles tell us that the shorter the time between the event and the response, the stronger the learning. The younger the child is, the more important timeliness becomes. Consider what would happen if, when you stuck your finger into a burning candle, you didn't feel the result until an hour later. Or, if you ate ice cream, the taste registered the next day. Consequences are most effective if they are immediate.

Timeliness is more important than severity. A very effective discipline device for young children is the "time out." You might place your child in a special chair when they have acted in a way that you want to discourage. Give a warning, but remember: once you give a warning, you cannot fail to follow through.

10. The tough-minded parent supplies as much background, tradition, and "roots" about the family as is feasible.

Continuity with the past and present members of the extended family is a powerful factor in providing positive feelings about life, the family, and the children themselves. While there are a number of potential problems looming for Japanese families as they seem to emulate many Western values, the continuity with ancestors and existing members of their extended families is a powerful stabilizing benefit.

The mature person does not live in the present alone but has a vision of the past and the future as well. The ability to see the past as having been made up of real people helps make it possible to see the lessons of the past as having real meaning for today and tomorrow. It helps to create a vision of the future as being real, something that will actually happen.

Who one is, one's sense of being, is strongly influenced by an awareness of the family of the present, the past, and the future. Identity is formed in relation to other people; the greater the human context within which the child's identity is seen, the more complete and healthy is the self-image.

We hope for our children to have wide horizons, to view themselves as a part of a whole nation and world of people and events. The ability to look beyond one's self includes the ability to look beyond the present time and to learn from it.

When I was a Little Girl

My grandmother grew up in a mining town in Montana in the 1880s. One of our most cherished memories is listening to her tell stories of the mountains, the miners, the wildlife, the Indians, and the adventures of her and her brothers. In her words, "I don't know how my mother ever stood it; we were always into something, and there was a lot to get into!" She told of her mother teaching them to respect Chinese immigrants; of lying down in the field when chased by a range steer and playing dead until the steer got tired of you and went away; of following an overheard hunter's directions to the den of a mountain lion; of playing in a abandoned, and forbidden, mine and returning to find it had caved in; of teaching in a frontier schoolhouse as a young woman; of a brother who went to join the Navy and never was heard from again. We heard of another brother who became lost to alcoholism. We heard of the relatives who founded a town in Minnesota. We heard of her, at age twenty, taking her friends' dares and walking across a narrow sluice a hundred feet in the air to prove how good her balance was.

We finally prevailed on her to write her story. She began the written version with "To you, those days are only ashes, but to me they are living coals." She then told of her very earliest childhood recollection, at age two, of being lost most of a day in a meadow while the whole community looked for her.

To us, now, these memories are "living coals," and serve as a point of comparison when we feel that we have hardships to deal with. Though long deceased, she is a role model for us all.

---

11. The tough-minded parent is perceived as a concerned parent rather than a worried or angry one.

Valid and informed concern can transmit a loving and unifying effect. By contrast, worry and anger irritate, diffuse, and bewilder.

12. The tough-minded parent believes the family member is right until and unless proven wrong.

This central practice must pervade all relationships if the tough-minded principles in this book are to be truly effective. Loving trust is a tangible symbol of tough-minded love in action, and it pays to do your best to keep track of what your child is doing. Constant suspicion and negative anticipation on the other hand stimulate behavior that appears to validate, and then to reinforce, further negative behavior.

The following examples are parents' statements from some actual court cases. In each case, parents usually assumed that the child was going to do wrong.

"I have always made him count out the change in my hand to make sure he didn't steal any money. Good thing, too, because here he is for shoplifting." (*How did this child come to believe he might be a thief?*)

"I always know he's going to lie!" (*What lessons has he learned about telling the truth? How was telling the truth rewarded in the past? Has he learned from the parent's reactions that it is actually safer for him to lie?*)

"I said to her: 'You look like a slut! Is that what you are trying to be?'" (*Might there have been an innocent reason for experimenting with a brighter lipstick?*)

"I told her she was going to flunk. She doesn't care about anything. She doesn't know anything." (*What's happening at school? Can she read? Can she see the chalkboard? Can she think clearly after being kept up all night listening to a fight or worrying over something?*)

"You seem to like talking dirty." (*Where did he learn these words? Does he know what they mean? Have you discussed in the family why you don't want them used?*)

If you expect the worst, you get it. If you extend reasonable trust, assuming the best, you'll more likely be pleased with what you see.

13. The tough-minded parent encourages a family lifestyle dedicated to physical, mental and spiritual fitness.

Fitness is another way of saying that the "toolbox" we carry on our shoulders must contain tools that are usable and workable. When we don't feel well, we don't think and act well. Thus, our example loudly shouts a message of passivity, lack of self-control, low energy, and a general failure to inspire followership. Again, the "use it or lose it" principle applies.

Breathless

I am not a paragon of virtue when it comes to fitness. Still, I have a habit of taking walks, using the stairs when I have a choice, and doing something outside regularly. Our juvenile court office was three blocks from the courthouse, and I often escorted adolescents, and sometimes their parents, to hearings. It is my habit to walk briskly. Though far from athletic, I arrived at the courthouse able to carry on a normal conversation. The youth, supposedly in the physical prime of life, was nearly always out of breath. I believe there was a correlation between their failure to keep reasonably fit and their other difficulties. (*Observations of a juvenile court officer.*)

14. The tough-minded parent realizes that every thought, word, or action either builds or destroys. They are committed to enhancement of all family members in all feasible ways.

Since no one can live in neutral for even a moment, it is crucial to target a life-style which enhances others throughout the day. When we fail to do this, the void is invariably filled by thoughts or actions which diminish. We cannot live in neutral! Life does not exist in neutral!

"Let's see your muscle, boy! Come on, let's see it. You call that a muscle? Look! Here's a real muscle." (*Someday, if he adopts the attitude taught by that example, and when he's big enough, he may show you some muscles in a way you won't like! Why?*)

"I tried to motivate him to really want to make the team. I tried to shame him into it. I finally said, 'You just don't have the guts!' And he doesn't." (*Where did he learn to feel inadequate?*)

"Oh, no! Not another one of your crazy ideas!" (*Crazy ideas—is there anything you use every day that wasn't a crazy idea sometime? Hope for your child to get crazy ideas! What happens to the joyful light of a child's inventiveness when it is stamped out each time it flares?*)

Tough-minded parents enjoy empowering their kids. They believe that people who are empowered have a clear understanding of their authority, responsibility, and accountability, and of their valued role in the family.

Tough-minded parents give earned praise unstintingly. The parent who feels that too much praise will make the child conceited or difficult is all too common, and tragic. Please note that we say earned praise, combined with unconditional love. Earned praise can seldom be overdone. It is the stuff of unity, growth, development, confidence, and *joy*!

15. The tough-minded parent realizes that skill and firmness in asking or expecting will accomplish more than ordering or directing.

Let's concede immediately that occasions do arise with the young child when they must be told to do something. We have already mentioned that certain dangers call for no-choice directives, especially for young children. As time goes by, however, it is very important to ultimately reach a level of insight when the power of asking over telling becomes understood, internalized, and practiced. The acid test is simply this: How do you like to be told to do something? And, how do you respond?

For Family Discussion

Some expectations are more important than others in terms of calling for a response. The following list is a proposed "hierarchy of expectations," ranging from those that must be met without question to those that you'd like to see but won't lose much sleep over. What expectations are there in your family that you would place in these categories? Are there some different categories you'd like to use?

The "instant obedience" category—expectations that must be met right now, every time, no questions asked, based on physical safety.

The "moral imperative" category—expectations based on values held by the family to be very important.

The "organizational imperative" category—expectations that the family members must meet in order for the family and household to function and their basic needs be met.

The "achievement" category—expectations having to do with family standards of performance.

The "druthers" category—expectations that are minor annoyances if not met.

What would happen if *all* expectations were placed in the first category? or the first two categories?

Are some expectations negotiable and some nonnegotiable?

Would you rather be asked? It's a matter of dignity. Requesting, asking, and expecting is an art to be studied, practiced, honed, and improved all of our lives. All of us can grow in this skill as long as we live.

16. The tough-minded parent is interested in continuous learning and growing, and the family knows it.

In the book, *Tough-Minded Leadership*, Joe Batten says that people follow a learner rather than a knower.

When the parent says by word and action, "I *know* because I'm your mother (or father)," this discourages sharing. Parenthood doesn't bestow automatic wisdom. It ought to bestow humility. A child might reasonably ask: "Is it true that all you have to do to know everything is to beget children?"

Spontaneity connotes realness. Warmth thaws and dissolves rigidly, hesitancy, and defensiveness. Genuine spontaneity stimulates working together for the mutual good of the family. It is an intrinsic factor in growth, acceptance, and learning.

17. The tough-minded parent strives for openness and vulnerability.

The open mind grows. The closed mind dies! When children perceive a parent as being open, growing, changing, and learning, they will be stimulated to do likewise. Such a parent is also much more approachable. Such relationships lend themselves to shared meaning and shared understanding, which is the definition of tough-minded communication.

Things which open grow. Things which close become weak and die. The very process of vulnerably reaching, stretching, and risking, causes the person to grow and become stronger. Closed, "safe," antiseptic, defensive thoughts and practices invariably weaken one's responsive capacity. And responsiveness is central to the tough-minded family.

Little children have a tendency to see their parent as all powerful. That view enhances the young child's sense of security in a very big world. As children grow, however, their need changes and the parent is a role model for what they will become. The parents who attempt to portray an omnipotent, invulnerable image will doom their child to automatic failure, for that ideal cannot be attained.

The tough-minded parent is tolerant of sincere mistakes and even makes deliberate a point of helping children realize that they, the parents, have human frailties and fallibilities.

The ability to laugh at yourself is usually an indication of mental health and can greatly facilitate effective communicating. You cannot

---

When my husband died, leaving me in charge of three young children, I thought I had to be very strong, very competent, superorganized, and always have everything done just right. As a blind person, and especially as a blind parent, I had already developed the ability to be highly organized. I also knew how to adopt the "I can do it" attitude and the "I am in charge" role. In short, I knew how to seem invulnerable to anything that might come my way.

It was my mistaken notion that this was what my children needed most during this time. My husband, who had also been blind, had been a full-parenting partner, and his loss was felt tangibly as well as emotionally. There was a lot more work to be done. For some reason, I also thought that the kids would be as scared as I was and that the best way to deal with this was for me to show absolutely no fear. I felt that the kids needed to know that all was in order, and that Mom was in control!

I was 100 percent wrong. After a few weeks of this, my adopted son shut himself in his room for several hours. I finally called him out and "competently" asked him what was wrong. He exploded! "We've lost more than a father around here!" he said. "We've also lost a *mother*! If you want to be sure your socks match, and that there are hot meals, or if you want everything organized, boy, we've got it. But, if you come home early because Mom might appreciate some company, or might need a shoulder to lean on, we don't have that."

I lost a lot of sleep that night and readily concluded that he was right. The children needed for me to show some of the "cracks in the rocks," that I was certainly feeling, and some softness. I had fooled myself into thinking that they needed me to be invulnerable. It was just the opposite.

Blind parents learn how to hear physical events around them very well. We always know what's happening in the house. Also, I already knew that I needed to listen carefully to what the kids were saying as well as to what they were doing. I had just been shocked out of it by my husband's death. My children brought me back to reality. Be real—be human—be vulnerable.

fool your children. Children know their parents have various weaknesses anyway, and the unattainable practice of rigidly depicting yourself as perfect will keep them at a distance or tempt them to see you as a fool. A contrived pedestal is a lonesome and unproductive place. On the other hand, "spoofing" yourself invites sharing. Besides all that, it's fun!

What mistakes have you made, and what lessons are in them for your children?

18. The tough-minded parent realizes that major family decisions will be largely counterproductive if not preceded by family involvement.

As we become involved, we share. We feel a part of the final decision. When the questions and opinions of children are sought, and often acted upon, they feel some "ownership" in the final decision. They feel like a family rather than a number of emotionally compartmentalized, disparate persons.

Involving the children in family decisions does not mean giving them an equal vote. What you seek is their real input into the decisions that affect them. There will be some questions that can be voted on and some that the children can decide alone, but parental wisdom must sometimes override children's desires. We can't expect ten-year-olds to have the perspective of an adult.

For Family Discussion

Many families hold a regular family council, perhaps weekly or semi-weekly. At the family council some decisions are made, a lot of ideas and opinions are exchanged, and everyone has a good time along with it.

What advantages can you see to holding a regular family council? What disadvantages?

What might be the rules at a family council?

What might be the rights of each family member?

What decisions can a family council make?

What decisions, if any, need to be reserved to the parent?

---

19. The tough-minded parent encourages ongoing discussions of family values and beliefs.

The value of any person is the sum of the values between their ears. Further, the value of a family is the sum of the values it holds and practices. Therefore, to effectively evaluate people, situations, opportunities, and circumstances, the tough-minded parent continuously seeks to identify, clarify, and internalize positive values. The term "evaluate" means, by definition, "to judge or determine the worth or quality of; appraise." Thus, the total capacity of the family to make more effective use of evaluative skills in every dimension of their lives will increase in direct proportion to the excellence and relevance of their values—their focus on *strengths*.

For Family Discussion

What does it mean to say: "Values answer the question, 'Why'?"
What are the values in your family?
Where do they come from?
How are they different from values found in other families?
Your parents' families?

There are lessons that families can learn from successful business. One is the importance of purpose.

Studies show that every successful enterprise, from a one-person store to a giant corporation, does best if it has a clearly understood purpose. Those companies that have most clearly stated their purpose in writing, that have involved everyone in developing their statement of purpose, and that constantly refer back to it as the basic guide to their actions, are those that thrive.

We suggest that you try to develop a statement of purpose with your family. State your beliefs and values. Define your goals. Talk about how your purpose and goals connect with what you believe in. We include as Appendix A some guidelines developed by Stephen R. Covey on "Personal and Family Mission Statements." We recommend it!

For Family Discussion

Faith

Your family values make your family special. Values rooted in a family spiritual life will make your family more special still. As you talk together about your goals, your family mission, and the beliefs and values that those are drawn from, consider these questions:

What does our family believe *purely on faith*?

What do we *know* is true and right whether anyone else agrees or not?

What do we know is the unseen truth that lies behind the world that we can see?

What does that faith mean to us a guide to our family mission, vision, values, goals, and actions?

Values and beliefs are not just for vague reference and wishful thinking. They are the basis of a successful plan for life.

20. The tough-minded parent fosters laughter and humor in all feasible ways.

Wholesome and positive laughter is a wonderful elixir, a balm for many family ills. It lightens and whisks the tensions away. Funny things happen constantly, usually based on a human "bumble" of some kind. In order to be ready for laughter, two ingredients are needed:

1. Ability to see the ridiculous in yourself and to let others enjoy a laugh at your expense. We all have silly mistakes, habits, and fumbles.

2. Readiness to drop your inhibitions. We can have the joy of uninhibited, funny behavior with the additional pleasure of being fully in touch with what's happening. We all have the ability to act foolish, if we are secure enough to let down our guard, and laugh.

21. The tough-minded parent believes that "expecting the best" of self and children is the only viable alternative.

The other alternative, expect the worst, which is now at epidemic proportion throughout the land, is unacceptable. We will not always get exactly what we expect from our children. We may not know exactly what we ought to expect. Our children's best may come in forms we would not have predicted or even imagined. If we expect our children to be the best, we may be surprised at how they express their best; but we will never be disappointed.

Try it.

10

Special Families and Special Problems

More and more, as we work with individual families or talk to groups of parents, we find ourselves confronted with a parent who says: "I'm a single parent," or, "I'm just divorced," or, "My wife (or husband) is an alcoholic. What do I do?"

Parents today are raising their children in many different kinds of family circumstances that call for special consideration. Also, there are many events that can happen in the raising of a child in any kind of family that deserve special attention.

Singles

About one-fourth of the children in America are now in single parent homes. This may be due to the untimely death of a spouse; it might be because of a divorce or other separation; it may result from a serious illness that debilitates one of the partners; it may be simply a matter of the parent choosing to remain single. Whatever the reason, single parenting is a fact for a large and growing portion of the children in our society, and there is no reason to believe that there will be any reversal of the trend soon. So what does the single parent do?

We believe that the greatest variable in parenting has more to do with the maturity, the capability, and the loving skills of the parent than with how many parents there are. Still, even a really tough-minded parent can be lonely, confused, and frightened when faced with raising children alone.

What should be our attitude toward single parents? What should the single parent's attitude be toward their child and the world around them? What is your attitude?

Single When Death Occurs

The opposite of death is life! When you are raising children and your partner dies, it seems that the whole world has crashed. Many of us face the death of a spouse while raising our children; any of us could. What do we go through?

After the initial period of learning to accept the death, and going through the various healthy and necessary phases of grief, we must adjust to a totally new situation. We discover how much we depended on our partner for attention, affection, advice, or as a sounding board. We discover how many ordinary chores were performed by the partner. We are very likely to discover how much we depended on their income. We will learn how much we leaned on their support and their simply being there for us.

At the same time, however, we discover new inner strengths that might otherwise never have surfaced. It's crucial to deal with your grief; if not for yourself, then for the children. If you have trouble reaching out to them in a loving and understanding way, you can contact a pastor or grief counselor for help for you and your children.

The adjustments to being alone are difficult enough for a parent without children or whose children are not at home. But when a parent is left with children, the phrase "life goes on" takes on urgent new meaning. Children can't wait.

Children do not stop needing to grow just because someone has died. Change does not cease. In fact, it's the business of children in the world to do just the opposite, to vigorously grow and replace those who pass on. Some children will hardly pause in their growth after the death of a parent. Other children, however, may have problems adjusting and may hesitate in their development. When a child loses someone particularly close, the child may even regress to an earlier pattern of behavior. Children need plenty of special nurturing, attention, and acceptance of their feelings during this period of time.

Any event in human life, even a tragedy, can be an opportunity to grow; there is even growth to be gained in death. It can often be a unique opportunity for human emotional development. Death is real. All people must face it. Because of this, we come equipped with human emotional responses that can carry us through this experience and allow us to benefit from it. We only run into trouble when we try to resist our natural reactions to death or when we allow it to debilitate us.

This is a time for honesty. Be honest with yourself about your feelings, and share this with the children. Allow yourself to grieve as hu-

---

Applying the Pledge

The death of a parent, or of anyone close to the family, is an opportunity to exercise several points of the "Pledge of the Tough-Minded Parent," and to grow.

"Share fully in our lives together." "Be *truthful and honest*." "Share, love, laughter, and life with my children." The operative word is *share*. Share with them the fact of the death and how you feel about it. You may feel sad, angry, afraid, even relieved that it's finally over. It's all right for your children to know this. It's all right for them to know that the death is hard for you to handle, that you also feel scared, hurt, lonely and sad.

Remind the children that you still love them unconditionally. Coming "completely unglued" may frighten very young children into feeling that they have lost not only the person who passed on, but may lose you as well.

Crying together after a death is healthy. Give your children the opportunity to grieve. Even laughter at the time of death can be healthy. Just because someone has died doesn't mean ridiculous things don't keep happening. Laugh, especially, at things the deceased would have laughed at. It's one loving way of continuing to share your life and your children's lives with them.

"The highest vision and values" come into focus at a time of crisis. Here is one of the best chances you will ever have to share with your child your belief system, your sense of the past and the future, your vision of hope.

Will your children come to view death as the futile end of futile living? Or will they review with you the good of the life that was lived?

Will they see the permanent contribution of the life just passed, even if only to see themselves as a lasting result of that life?

Will they live in debilitating fear of death? Or, on the other extreme, might they live in ignorance of it and lose, thereby, appreciation for the life they have?

mans need and are uniquely able to do, and help your children to do the same. Accept all your feelings as good, and allow the children to do the same. Then, move on into life. It's all right even to feel relief over the passing of a loved one. There may be some feeling of guilt. Deal with it; don't set it aside. If these feelings persist or keep you from functioning, consider counseling for yourself and the children.

Finally, the person who died wasn't perfect. Even the finest person you ever knew was a nuisance in some ways. We all are. There is nothing wrong with relief that you don't have to deal with the ordinary irritations that go along with living with anyone, even though maybe you'd gladly do it to have them back. Children are often less constrained in stating such things and may express their relief that they don't have to put up with some irritating habit the dead person exhibited. Listen to them without "correction." Help them to understand that this feeling, too, is all right.

Keep in touch with your network. You are still a parent; you may still have parents, cousins, and friends. They still need you, and you need them. They will still enjoy you, and you can still enjoy them. Lengthy isolation is to be avoided. Life is still there—*live!*

Clearly, a parent who is suddenly left alone to raise children has a demanding job. The adult chores may all fall to one person. In most instances, the parent is working. Get help! Where? From each other! Children of any age will feel good about making a meaningful contribution to the family. Share with them the list of things that need to be done and help them to select ways in which they can really help.

Time may seem to be more limited. But, in at least one way, there is more time than before: the time you were spending with your spouse is now available for you. Use this time to your advantage. Spend it with the children and with yourself!

The opposite of death, and its unfailing antidote, is life!

Single When Divorce Occurs

Increasing individual choice in life is one of the most powerful trends in history. Increasing choice about getting married and staying married is a part of this history. Until fairly recently, marriage was forever. Most marriages were preplanned by families. Many times the choice of part-

---

Herb

Kids need, and will find, adult role models outside the home. Even when there are two parents available, someone else to learn from is vital to full personal development. When there is only one parent, this becomes even more important.

There is a scoutmaster named Herb. Herb is a real person. Herb can tie knots, build a fire, cook outside, make a rope bridge, find his way, and hike most people a fourth of his age to exhaustion. He is clean spoken. He encourages advancement in the scout ranking system and usually gets it. Like most people, he has a distinctive way of standing, speaking, and dressing with distinct body language and facial expressions. He is not, and does not pretend to be, perfect but makes errors and laughs about them. He seeks help in those areas where his skills are not best suited to the demand and usually gets it. He is stubborn about basic principles.

For some reason, a lot of boys without fathers, or fathers who are not fully engaged, join Herb's troop. But those boys with fully involved fathers enjoy him just as much, partly because their fathers do.

If you send your boy to a week of camp with Herb, he will come back using Herb's language patterns, Herb's ways of standing and walking, Herb's body language and facial expressions, and Herb's values.

"Herbs" are available in the form of men and women all over the country. The YWCA-YMCA; the Brownies and Girl Scouts; the Campfire; the 4-H, Sunday School; Big Brothers-Big Sisters; the chorus; the track team; baseball and soccer teams; the drama coach; the retired neighbor who putters in the yard, bakes, tats, or fixes things.

Make sure of the character and value system of anyone you turn your child over to, then *use them.*

---

ner was made without the consultation, let alone the consent, of the partners. Gradually, however, marriage has become entirely a matter of the conscious choice of the partners, with little input from anyone else.

For a couple of centuries in the Western world, marriage by choice has been the norm. Until recent decades the idea prevailed that once people made the choice to get married they were expected to make it work. There were very few accepted reasons for divorce. Now, however, divorce is legally easy. Marriage dissolution, like marriage itself, has become just another matter of individual choice. Regardless of whether the trend is considered to be positive or negative, no one can question the fact that most people are now free to enter and to leave the married status at will. And so, they do. Half of all United States marriages end in divorce.

Matter of choice or not, separation is a highly traumatic time for everyone. In many ways, it may be more stressful to lose a spouse to divorce than to lose one to death. One reason for this is that in divorce there is a sense of personal failure. There may be a self-suspicion that, somehow, you could have made it work or at least have made a better choice in the first place. There is also less sense of having been rejected by the partner who has passed away.

Divorce very often includes a highly charged contest, a full-scale battle waged across the bedroom, the living room, the dining room, the children's room, and the courtroom. Anger and resentment occur over the most trivial possession. Often, children see that their separating parents make more fuss over a television set or stereo than they do about where the children will have their home. What can they conclude from this about their own importance?

Death and divorce are, however, alike in that they both consist of a major personal loss. Grief is the common denominator of the two experiences. Something that was once there is gone. A set of dreams. A feeling of being wanted, trusted, and needed. A piece of identity. A place with memories and things in it that was "home." Each parent feels these losses. So does each child.

In death, the break is complete, at least so far as this life is concerned. But, when you have children, the divorce is never really final. The relationship that produced the children is carried on in them, and nothing can change that fact. Children, emotionally, will always wish their parents were together, and many of their actions will reflect that. They may accuse, rebel, go back to earlier childhood behaviors, become physically ill. Parents must remember: the children have suffered a loss, too, and they must also grieve. Their feelings of fear, anger, shame, and guilt are real and must be respected.

Children in a divorce situation are never really willing to fully choose

Mom and Dad Won't Be Staying Together Any More

Here are some steps each parent can take to help children through the divorce.

1. Decide whether your child is important enough to you to avoid making him as just another means of waging war with your expartner.

2. Avoid "bad-mouthing" your partner. It won't work, because eventually the child will try to find out if you were telling the truth. Children are the most underrated lie detectors in the world.

Instead of harming your partner, you are pulling out part of the foundation of the child's world. If your expartner has been abusive, addictive, or has other real problems, explain this to the children in terms of the partner needing help and you needing to have protection.

3. Do share with the children what is happening. The truth will seem less traumatic to the child than the explanation they will conjure up in their imagination or what they may hear from others. Let them know especially what is going to happen to them. This ought to be done by the parents together if possible; often, an impartial mediator can help in these discussions. We encourage you to seek help for the children during this time.

4. Try very hard to keep the partner involved in the child's life, and keep yourself involved. Don't make that involvement an excuse to badger your expartner. Even if attempts to communicate about the children deteriorate into a "bad scene," don't give up. Hopefully, the time will come when the need to ventilate anger will subside and it will be possible to focus discussion on the children.

5. Review the "Pledge" daily, and try to do something that exemplifies each point once with your children during each day.

6. Take adult rights and responsibilities seriously. Adults, at least one but usually two, have made the choice to break the marriage; let those who make the choice put as little of the price on the innocent as possible.

7. "What if I just can't get the other parent to cooperate?" If you have sought truly impartial, informed, competent advice, and the opinion is that the other parent is truly doing harm to the children, ask your legal adviser to find ways to minimize that parent's involvement with the children. But, be sure you are right when you take this drastic, and potentially harmful, step.

between their parents. If the children are minors, though, someone will choose for them which parent they will be living with. They will be forced to change households. Even if they stay in the same physical home, the absence of one parent makes it a strange place in many ways.

There are beginning to be support groups for children from divorce situations. We encourage you to seek help for your child, and for yourself.

Single By Choice

"Do not judge or you too will be judged" (Matt. 7:1).

Singles are not a new phenomenon in the world. Nor are single parents so rare in history. Clearly, though, there are more women today choosing to keep a baby and more people choosing to adopt children and raise them alone. Many of these adopted children are hard-to-place children who would otherwise have no home at all.

We are, in this book, dealing with the real world of parenting as we find it. In that world, many young people are making a single parent choice. The reasons for this choice are as many as the number of situations. Some of those reasons may seem wise and some not so wise. We feel that the team arrangement of two tough-minded parents has a better chance of working, but we know of single parents, due to every kind of circumstance, who are raising their children well. Whatever the circumstance, accept your children enthusiastically and vulnerably.

APPLYING THE PLEDGE

1. Accept your children enthusiastically and vulnerably. If you know any single parents, recognize the special efforts they face, admire the courage they have to make this choice. It isn't necessary to agree with everything other people do to accept them as worthwhile individuals.

2. If you are a single parent, how do you see yourself? How do you assume the world sees you? A chip on your shoulder will not help you to gain acceptance. Instead of assuming that you will *not* be accepted, go about in confidence that you *will* be. This expectation will be fully met among the people you care about most, because you will inspire it. You need to be able to accept yourself before being concerned about whether others will accept you.

3. Love the children of the single parent as you love any other children. Be a part of their supportive, helping network.

4. Encourage single parents to make use of the many networks that exist; be a "Herb," or help them to find one.

5. Ask, listen, and hear the single parent. They have a unique experience to share, and you can learn much from them. Like most people, they usually welcome advice and help when they are ready for it.

6. If you are a single parent, don't shun the wisdom available to you from other parents. "Asking, listening, and hearing will lead to acceptance, communication, growth, and access to the knowledge that everyone raising children needs.

For Family Discussion

How does a fifteen-year-old mother decide about carrying her baby to term?

What happens if a fifteen-year-old mother keeps her baby?   What does it mean to be a fifteen-year-old mother?

What are most fifteen-year-olds who are not parents doing in their fifteenth year? sixteenth? seventeenth? eighteenth?

What if a fifteen-year-old father marries the mother?

What if a fifteen-year-old father desires that the baby be carried to term?

What does it mean to be a fifteen-year-old father?

How does one get to be a mother or father in the first place?

What is adoption all about?

Adoption

Adopted children have some special advantages and face some special problems. The vast majority of infant adoptions work out very well. Adoptive services and procedures vary somewhat from state to state. They all have in common that a person or agency trained and licensed in adoptions will work with the couple desiring to adopt. This person will typically visit and approve the adopting family and advise them as to the unique nature of adopting a child. An important part of this is ensuring that the extended family will welcome the adoptive child as well as the new parents will.

Meanwhile, the agency, or in many instances an attorney who specializes in adoptions, will be aware that there is a couple looking for an infant or other child. The agency or attorney may hear of a mother who is going to bear a child and is considering surrendering the child for adoption. Laws in every state now protect natural parents very well in assuring that they have every opportunity to consider, and reconsider, giving their child up for adoption.

Adoptive children may have special needs and special advantages. Adoptive children have an opportunity to feel especially loved because there is no doubt that they were wanted by their adopted parents. They also can fall prey to the concern that they were rejected by their natural parents, and are therefore less "good" than other children.

A central issue in adoptions today is whether the adoptive child should be able to seek and find the natural parents. Complicating this is the question of whether the natural parent's desire not to be known outweighs that of the child's desire to know them. Many legislators, courts, social agencies, and associations of adoptive parents and children are struggling with this thorny issue. As in many family-related situations, there is a clear conflict of rights with genuine arguments of compassion on each side.

It is clear, though, that adoptive children and their adoptive parents should be furnished with as much factual information about the natural parents as possible. Family medical histories are vital, as there are genetically transmitted physical problems that physicians need to know about. It is also helpful to know something about the family's physical tendencies, height, hair color, eye color, tendency to sunburn. Increasingly, it is felt to be of interest and importance to know of addictive tendencies in the family histories.

Adoption works. Families can be successfully completed through adoption to the benefit of both the parents and the child. The joy of bringing home an adoptive baby or child is fully as great as bringing home your own biological infant. The key to a successful adoption is that adoptive parents accept the children as though they were their own. They, in fact, *are* their own.

Love makes the bond.

Insight for Blind Parents

Outstanding on our panel of experts was our H.O.P.E. team member, Revanne Ducket, a tough-minded parent who has experienced the adoption of step-children, the birth and raising of two children, and the death of a spouse. She is also blind, as was her husband, and gave us many useful tips for blind parents. We will tell parts of her story here, including anecdotes from her life as a child, a wife, a professional person, and a mother.

"Children have been at the center of our home since the day I was married. On that day I acquired a husband, a house, and two adorable, five-year-old Korean step-children. On the day of our wedding, my husband-to-be called to ask if I would like to have the children to take to the church with me: they were bathed, dressed and ready to go, and he could stand a few minutes of peace and quiet to get ready. I was thrilled at the prospect, and Mom and I picked them up in a few minutes. A problem immediately arose as we realized that all of us and my dress would not fit into her car. Since I am blind and do not drive, I made a quick dash to the phone and called a cab, explaining to the dispatcher what the problem was: I needed to be at the church in less than half an hour for the wedding. The short taxi ride with two exuberant children bouncing up and down and offering their rendition of 'Here Comes the Bride' was an experience to be remembered.

"We have the album of wedding pictures, but nowhere is there to be found a paper print of those moments when I feel we truly became a family. Those images are engraved in my heart. As we approached our home after the wedding, to my surprise and delight, my husband, Warren, scooped me up in his arms. The front steps were wide and therefore no problem, but then came the dilemma of fitting us and the wide hoop of my wedding dress through a normal-size front door. We finally made it, and Warren deposited me laughing in the center of our living room. I sank to the carpet, and Tracy and Todd scampered across my dress for our first real hug as a family.

"Since that day in 1966, the privileges, responsibilities, and challenges of parenthood have provided a continuous learning experience for me. We took Tracy to the airport to return to her mother, and Todd stayed with us. Warren obtained permanent custody of Todd, and later through adoption he legally became my eldest son. In 1967 his brother Dana was born, and seventeen months later Stephen arrived.

"In our busy household, it was easy to misunderstand what someone was trying to communicate. I learned early to hear not merely what one of our sons was saying but to understand what he meant. For many years there was a plaque in our home that defused many potentially dangerous situations and set us back in the direction of real communication. It read: "I know you believe you understand what you thought I said, but . . . ."

"As a blind parent I used many alternative techniques, including braille, a long white cane, and more intensive reliance on my other senses. Of course, our home was "childproofed," but that did not change the fact that I needed to know where the children were and what they were doing. The uniqueness of each child meant that just when I began to think I knew a little about parenting it was time for a new strategy or technique.

"There were, though, a few basics that remained unchanged. Diapering baby meant that all necessary items needed to be within my reach but out of the way of waving arms and kicking feet. I was surprised to discover how far a twenty-inch-long baby could reach! At spoon-feeding time a finger under baby's chin not only guided the spoon in my other hand to the mouth in need, but also warned when he was going to turn his head, clamp his mouth shut, or fling out a little arm. Bells attached to shoelaces made easy trackers fur busy toddlers.

"It was also necessary to establish that, while we would rarely say "No!" or "Stop! in authoritative tones, there was to be no argument when we did say these words.

"Todd entered kindergarten at the nearby school. (On that first day of school, I could have no idea how much that school and its understanding staff would come to mean to our family as we progressed through the growing years and the later struggle of Warren's illness and death when Stephen had just turned seven.) When Dana was born, Todd invited his new classmates over to see "his" new baby. I think every child in the school must have come! Many friends had warned us that Todd would be jealous of the new baby. I shared this concern with my physician, and he said, "Are you really planning to let that happen?" Todd and Grandma picked out the suit for Dana to wear home from the hospital. Todd was the first to hold him when we arrived home. Grandma had to wait, but she recovered. Todd picked out the first toy. It was a fluffy white lamb with a bell in its ear so I could keep track of it.

"I never really doubted that I could successfully raise children. Warren never let blindness limit his ambitions. As I was growing up, I was not aware that a blindness was a handicap. My mother never told me it was! I remember doing needlework in kindergarten; the teacher said to thread the needle, so I threaded it. It was much later that I learned that the rest of the kids were using their eyes for this operation. I didn't know I couldn't do it, so I did it.

"One of the statements that guides me throughout my life is this: Argue for your limitations, and sure enough they are yours. We ask not, Can it be done by a blind person, but, How can it be accomplished? It is just a matter of developing alternative techniques and proceeding with self-confidence.

"Thus it was with raising my children. It was necessary, for instance, to know when they were trying to get by with something. They soon learned that I could hear the water running if they were sent to wash their hands; the next step was to check for the smell of soap. We often had other kids in. I learned the sounds made when any object in the house was moved no matter where in the house I was. 'Put that down, Johnny. We don't play with that.' One of the boys sneaked out of his window after hours. Rather than stay awake half the night waiting to see when he came home, I put a coffee can full of silverware on the window ledge; this made a really good clatter, and I didn't have to make any comment the next day on his outing. The outings ended.

"When my husband's struggle with cancer was leading to its inevitable conclusion, Warren wanted to be at home as long as possible. When told that he had perhaps two months to live, Warren said, 'Thank God, you can handle it.' Once I started to leave his bedside so I could regain control, but his firm hand pulled me back in the chair, and he said, 'Oh, no you don't, not this time; we are in this together and although I may not be able to do much else, I can be a shoulder for you to cry on if that's what you need.' We planned a family trip we knew he'd never share with us. Close to the end, we had a family prayer around the bed with Warren leading. He had no resonance to his voice by then, but his tone was thankful and caring. Each child took a turn offering part of a prayer, with the last child checking with me to see if he should end with the Lord's Prayer. Some times my children could say things when I was unable to. They took charge of gathering Daddy's favorite clothes to take to the funeral home."

Mrs. Ducket has been a leading figure at the Iowa Commission for the Blind. She presently works there as a volunteer, and works with groups of abusive parents in Des Moines. Both she and her mother are still tough-minded parents of the first magnitude.

Alcoholic Parent

It is estimated that one in every four children is from a home heavily impacted by an alcoholic. Many children have both parents who drink or are otherwise addicted. In many other instances, only one is so afflicted.

Children of alcoholics develop in characteristic ways. A common adjustment is to go to an extreme. Many children act out at school and elsewhere to attract attention. Others are just the opposite—they attempt to become invisible, hoping not to be noticed. Still others may believe that they are to blame for the parent's drinking and strive to make up for what they think is their own shortcoming. They may become extremely organized, become "super children," doing everything just right. Often, they are outstanding in school, achieving beyond their reasonable best. The common element is that they move toward an extreme.

Children of alcoholics may *look* all right. They are very good at performing according to what they think is expected. Don't let this facade of normalcy prevent you from seeking help for your child if he or she has lived with an alcoholic adult, especially a parent. In any case in which someone you love is addicted, you may want to seek help and advice from a treatment center or a substance abuse information center. The alternatives of voluntary treatment, intervention, and even involuntary commitment are available in various ways in most states. Become informed. Know as much as you can about what is happening to your family member. Act if you can.

What if treatment is refused or otherwise not an alternative that is within your control? If you are a parent, you must learn about how the alcoholism or other addiction of your spouse is affecting your child. *It always has a profound, harmful effect on children.* What are your choices?

1. Take your child and get out. If there is no hope for change in the near future, and it is within your practical ability to do so, remove yourself and the child from this damaging influence. Staying with an addicted person who will not seek help and who may be abusing or endangering you is of no help to them and is of harm to you and your child.

2. Seek support for yourself and your child. It is of the utmost importance that your child realize that she is not alone in this situation. Children tend to believe that this problem is somehow unique to them. It is of great help to them to be able to share with other children who are or have been in the same circumstances. It is of help to you, too. Contact a local treatment center or alcoholism authority to find out where support groups may be found.

3. If the spouse enters treatment, involve yourself and the child in the program. It is important to remember that the whole household has adjusted to the drinking behavior and now must take on a new pattern to support not drinking. Your child has become accustomed to dealing with the drinking and may find it difficult to adjust to the sobriety.

4. Become informed. Your local AA 12-Step service or any treatment center will have materials.

It is as vital to get information if you are a child of alcoholic parents as it is if you are a parent married to one. Your own experiences are still with you and will profoundly affect the ways in which you interact with children and your spouse.

According to the children of Alcoholics Foundation, Incorporated, one out of every eight Americans is the child of an alcoholic. Of the twenty-eight million children of alcoholics in the United States, seven million are under the age of eighteen. We know that:

- Alcoholism runs in families.
- Sons of alcoholic fathers are four times more likely to become alcoholics.

• Daughters of alcoholic mothers are three times more likely to become alcoholics.
  • Children of alcoholics are often grandchildren of alcoholics.
  • Daughters of alcoholics are more likely to marry alcoholics.

How do children of alcoholics feel?
  • Guilty and responsible for parental drinking and unaware that alcoholism is a disease which they cannot cause, control, or cure.
  • Invisible and unloved, since family life revolves totally around the alcoholic parent.
  • Insecure, due to consistent inconsistencies in parental behavior, attitudes, and rules.
  • Fearful that the alcoholic parent will become ill, have an accident, or die.
  • Embarrassed by the public behavior of alcoholic parents.
  • Ashamed because of the stigma society attaches to alcoholism and the need to keep it a family secret.
  • Frightened by family conflict, violence, and abuse.

How do children of alcoholics react?
As youngsters, children of alcoholics may be more likely to:
  • Have learning difficulties, do poorly in school, be truant or delinquent.
  • Have fewer friends.
  • Suffer psychosomatic illnesses.
  • Be victims of neglect, child abuse, or incest.

As teenagers, children of alcoholics may be more likely to:
  • Be expelled from school or drop out due to early marriage, pregnancy, institutionalization, or military enlistment.
  • Abuse alcohol or other drugs.
  • Have serious behavior problems, anxiety, or depression.
  • Attempt suicide.

As adults, children of alcoholics may be more likely to:
  • Have problems with interpersonal relationships.

- Experience difficulties in the workplace.
- Overuse medical facilities.
- Become alcoholic, suicidal, or mentally ill.

The Alcoholic Parent's Myths
- I'll quit tomorrow.
- I don't have a problem; I can stop any time.
- I can control it.
- I'll just have one more.
- I just like to have a good time.
- Of course I can drive—I've only had a few.
- It wasn't the job for me anyway.
- If you had my problems, you'd drink, too.
- It's not my fault that I drink.
- Nobody in this family understands me.
- If I got some love and affection, I wouldn't drink.
- I'm sorry.
- I promise.

The Nonalcoholic Parent's Myths
- Maybe he's not really an alcoholic.
- She can't be an alcoholic—she gets to work every day.
- Maybe he'll learn to control his drinking.
- Maybe next time she won't drink so much.
- How can I abandon someone who's sick?
- I'm sure I can help him.
- It's my fault she drinks.
- Maybe if I change, he'll stop drinking.
- If she loved, me, she'd stop.
- Maybe he'll leave me if he gets sober.
- If only. . .
- She promised . . .

The Child's Myths
- If he loved me, he wouldn't drink so much.
- It's all my fault.

- She didn't really mean to hurt me.
- Maybe if I'm good . . .
- Maybe I'm crazy . . .
- Maybe next time . . .
- If I'm strong, I can handle this.
- I don't need any help.
- I'll never end up like that.
- I have to take care of him.
- I make mountains out of molehills.
- If I behave, she won't drink so much.
- If she wasn't so mean, he wouldn't drink so much.
- It doesn't really matter.
- I'll try harder.
- But she promised me. . . .

Another Special Family—Yours!

Single parenting—death—adoption—blindness—alcoholism—are but a few of the many family situations of joy or difficulty to be found in any community. All can result in success for every family member if a positive, "We can do it and enjoy it" approach is taken.

Successful parenting depends very little on what the circumstances of your life happen to be but very much upon the value system that determines what you do with those circumstances.

11

What Do We Do When?
Parents' Nightmares

Emmett Fox said, "To be afraid is to have more faith in evil than in God" (New York: Harper and Brothers, 1940).

Every time we have talked about tough-minded parenting with a group of parents, we have received a number of "What do we do when...?" questions. The parents then usually describe some dilemma they have, such as children running away, emotional quarrels, teenage pregnancy, threats of suicide, or experimentation with alcohol.

Families don't exist in a dream world where everything is always "just fine." They never did. One might say, "Nowadays, you don't know what to expect." And that's true. There were big family problems and unexpected happenings in the past, but this is a unique age in its own way, just as the past times were each unique in theirs.

This chapter briefly describes some of the key parental concerns of our time and suggests ways in which parents might respond. If you are faced with serious problems, you may want to consult with your pastor, your school counselor, your police, or even a child mental health practitioner. Seeking help can sometimes be necessary, but don't surrender your own final responsibility for your children.

"I'm Going to Kill Myself"

Almost every adolescent knows someone who has either talked about or attempted suicide, and the odds are they know of someone who has been successful.

Many adults have trouble understanding the reasons for the rise in youth suicide. It should seem that there is more for a young person to live for today than ever before. There is no question that life is physi-

172

cally easier than ever and opportunities for success are tremendous. Still, adolescent suicide increases. Why? Interviews with teens who have made suicidal attempts or gestures or who have threatened suicide lead to these conclusions:

1. *Parents are so involved in their vocational or recreational lives that they do not have time to spend with the child.*—This leads to an incredible loneliness and sense of worthlessness. Children are logical: they can see that when money, career success, recreation, and luxury items absorb more attention than they do it means that these things are more important. If you are fourteen and you seem to be less important to your parent than the lawn, the business, the stereo, the addictive substance, the bowling team, the television program, or their current romantic interest, what do you have to live for? How can you discover what your own importance is to your parents? Suicide can be the ultimate attention-seeking device.

2. *Children have a longer way to go to gain their independence than ever before.*—If children drop out of school, they know that they will almost certainly never have anything in today's working world. Their choices are limited; they must stay in school, and do well at it, or fail for a lifetime. A few stumbles in school can seem like the end of the world and can seem like a cause to give up on living in it. Even a string of seemingly unbroken successes can be frightening to an adolescent. The child who surprises everyone with a suicide attempt because "they had everything going for them" may simply have run out of steam and become despairing of the continuing, endless struggle to meet their own unrealistic standard. They may be expecting perfection of themselves instead of expecting their best.

3. *Children have too little training and experience in handling their feelings and relationships.*—A broken romance can seem like the end of the world if the adolescent has invested her or his whole reason for being in that other person. Children who have little reason to feel good about themselves, who have not been convinced at home that they are consistently and unconditionally loved, are highly vulnerable to becoming overinvested in a relationship and more easily hurt when it ends.

4. *Children often have not developed a strong value system that em-*

phasizes life.—They can reasonably ask: "If the material world of manufactured goods is all there is, then of what value am I? If the 'here and now' is all there is, then why live into a future? If all we hear of the past is that it was miserable, why expect a better tomorrow? If the future is going to be as bleak and hopeless as the present, who wants it? If I have no awareness of the beauty and meaning of the past, why should I believe there is beauty and meaning now or that there will be in the future? We cherish and preserve those things that are valued, and discard those that are not—including ourselves.

5. *Suicide can become the "thing to do."*—All of us, and most particularly adolescents, are prone to imitate our peers. We look to them for approval and example. A suicide in a town or school draws a lot of attention. In every instance, there will be something in the life of the suicide victim that other teens can identify with, and say, "Hey! He was just like me!" Sometimes, the need for finding other people who will treat you as being important is so great that teens will form groups in which "suicide pacts" are made, and sometimes kept.

6. *Some rock music groups and videos present lyrics seeming to advocate or glorify suicide and even may realistically enact or depict it.* —Teens who are unsure of themselves may be particularly vulnerable to this music. They may even believe they are imitating an idol.

7. *To many teens, death is not permanent or even "real."*—Many adolescents who have attempted suicide testify they envisioned the death as painless and imagined the funeral as though they would be there to see it. They believe that they will, somehow, be able to take part in, or at least witness and draw some satisfaction from how everyone they know reacts to their death. They are looking for the affirmation they crave in life, but are not receiving. In the movies or on television, the actor who suffers a gruesome death is seen to be another character next week, and the death was just "for play." The finality of death is not real to a generation overly influenced by the fantasy media. In addition, it is a common characteristic of teens that they believe themselves to be indestructible.

Don't Fool with Suicide

If a child or adolescent talks about committing suicide or makes what seems like a suicidal gesture, take all necessary protective measures without delay. Call the police, a hospital, a family physician, or a psychiatric or psychological service immediately, and follow their instructions. Don't leave the person unattended. Remove dangerous objects, drugs, and car keys.

This is the time when your love and support are more important. You may need to take stock of your time investment and actions with your child. Work with your child's mental health professional to make whatever changes need to be made.

Many suicide experts state that boys more often succeed at suicide attempts than do girls. Boys will more often create a suicide plan that is likely to work and then carry it out with little warning. Girls will more often make warning calls to friends or leave notes well in advance stating what they plan to do and why. Boys more often use guns and cars; girls more often use pills or cut their wrists. Attempts with cars and guns are more likely to be successful because rescue or interference is almost impossible, but there is some chance of failure or of discovery and rescue with pills and slit wrists. Some boys and girls, however, follow neither of the above patterns. It is unsafe to predict in any given case what pattern a boy or girl will follow.

Running Away

"I'm leaving!" Parents hear these dreaded words pretty often from kids today. Sometimes, however, the teenager may leave without even saying a word.

We have already discussed the "streetwise" child, citing some of the reasons why children get into that life-style and why they often find it easy to stay in it. What we did not point out was that most children who run away come back home.

Most of the work done on runaway children concentrates on why they run away. It may be a warning sign of other serious problems. We believe that the practice of tough-minded parenting will reduce the likelihood that children will run away in the first place. Still, it can happen, and every parent has a good chance that it will happen to them.

Remember being a child? Didn't it seem that you had the least power of anyone? Someone else had control over everything: the food, the money, the place, the activities. Other people could make you do things and prevent you from doing things. How frustrating! The increasing desire for power over your own life is a vital part of growing up. When faced with powerlessness in a situation, it's not surprising that someone may consider leaving. Maybe you considered running away yourself as a child.

The parable of the prodigal son reminds us that there have always been attractive reasons to leave home. We also learn that the world can turn against you and that you may want to come back home. Most importantly, though, we learn that you can come back home.

Having a child run away hurts parents. It is a loss, and it causes grief. It leaves parents feeling angry, frightened, guilty, rejected, and unappreciated. All the feelings that go with any loss go with running away. The feelings are real, and we need to go ahead and feel them.

Having a child run away very often comes as a surprise. First, we may be surprised to find that there was anything to run away from. Second, we may be surprised to discover that our child has the ability to plan and carry out a run away in the first place.

"Don't let the door hit you on the way out!" is a frequent parental reaction to the rejection, anger, and the fear of finding that your child has left home. Such a reaction may be understandable, but it makes a hard policy to live with.

For Family Discussion

All healthy children leave home sometime.

Eventually, children leave for good. Running away is a kind of leaving without prior family planning. The child, and the parents, need to discuss ways of getting ready for the day when the child will become independent and move out. This important stage of life can become a part of the plan and something to look forward to for the future. You can help prepare for this time by taking advantage of good opportunities for your child to travel or visit outside the home.

The act of running away is not the end of the line! Let's consider these points about the runaway child.

1. Adolescents, make mistakes. So do parents. We learn from these

What Do We Do When? **177**

mistakes if we are willing to. Running away may call attention to a problem that we need to pay attention to, such as a need to communicate. Ask, listen, and hear.

2. Running away may teach the adolescent one of many lessons about learning to live on the outside world. A child may find and develop strengths from this experience that he could not find any other way. Parents can, too.

3. There will be another year and another forty years! You and your child are in the process of developing a relationship that will last for your lifetime. Is running away the act that must break that relationship forever? Or can it perhaps strengthen the relationship? How you respond can make the difference. Someday this event will be in the past. In the future you and your son or daughter very likely will look back and talk about this experience together, and even laugh about it.

4. Running away is exciting and fun, for the one running. That's not all it is, of course; it's also pretty frightening. But, we should not be surprised to know that two or more adolescents running away together will do a lot of laughing. Adolescents need adventure, and running away can provide this. While this does not excuse it (we think it's important that you take action), it may help to understand if your runaway has funny stories to tell when she comes back home. Even the prodigal son must have had some adventures to share after his return, and those less adventurous siblings who stayed home probably listened with a fair degree of envy.

5. Does your child know what being "away" is? Have they had this adventurous experience? Has your child had a chance to be away in healthy ways? Have they visited distant relatives? been to camp? Have they taken group excursions, such as with a church, school, or other organization? Have they travelled with the family of a friend?

6. Why do runaways come home? In the story of the prodigal son, the question seldom seems to be asked, "Why did he come back?" This may be because the answer is so obvious: he knew that he could. Would your child be accepted back into the family and forgiven after a running away?

7. Running away is dangerous. There is no doubt that the child is safer in your home (assuming you are not an abuser) than on the road.

There are plenty of very real dangers to be found. Parental fear for their runaway child is understandable and based on reality. Anger toward your child for putting you through such fear is also understandable. Some sort of "justice" in parental reaction when the child comes home is a reasonable expectation. Remember however, to emphasize first the joy that the family member is safe and back home, then take reasonable action. Discipline will have no meaning if there is no love behind it.

8. Ask for help. A missing child is a serious problem. You have the right to seek the assistance of the police. Sometimes you may have to insist to get their help. Try to put yourself in the place of the law enforcement officer who, on the same day that a parent calls about a runaway teenager, may be dealing with armed robberies, burglaries and other dangerous crimes. Try to understand that responding to "domestic" situations can be a real nuisance, especially since so many turn out to be false alarms. But, politely insist that they take your call and act on it. Your runaway needs to know that this is an act that is viewed as serious and dangerous.

For Family Discussion

What does it mean to "run" away?
What are some other kinds of being "away"?
Can you run away from something without ever physically leaving?
What is "away"?
Are you "away" when you are at school?
Are you "away" when you are on a trip with a friend?
Are you ever really "away" from your home?
Is it true that "absence makes the heart grow fonder'?
If so, how does that work?

Hello, Mom? Can You Get Me Out Of Jail?

Sometimes the answer is, "Yes." Sometimes it may be, "No."

Your son or daughter will live most of his or her life in the real "outside" world, not at home. There are some lessons that can only be taught be the world, not by *you*.

How many people reading this book have never engaged in an act for which they could have been arrested? If you can say that you never have, you are in a very distinct minority! Almost everyone has done something that was in violation of criminal statues. This usually happens when we are in our teens. It may consist of decorating someone's house with toilet paper or shoplifting a tempting item. It may mean sneaking into an abandoned house and looking around, stealing from an orchard, siphoning gasoline, buying beer illegally, sneaking into the theater, or punching someone in the nose.

Sometimes, when kids break the law, they get caught. When they do, they often have the very unpleasant experience of being taken to the police station, maybe fingerprinted, placed in a locked room, even treated gruffly by officers who have "had it with kids" for the day. The parents may then have the trying experience of going after their child in the middle of the night, followed by a second trip to the police station or the juvenile court to follow up on the incident. Crime is not to be taken lightly. The parent's reaction is justly a serious one. It is important, though, to realize that it is not the end of the world. Separate the act from the person." Here is the most important time, and one of the hardest times, to apply this rule in raising children.

"Look what you did to us!" "What will people think?" "Oh, where did we go wrong?" These are some typical statements made to children by parents when they bring them home from the jail. Try instead:

"This is not what our family believes in!"

"I feel very angry and hurt by this!"

"What you did was very wrong."

"I know that you did something really wrong, but I still believe in you. But understand this: I don't expect to see this again!"

Follow such a statement with a discussion of the changes you want to see and listen to suggestions the child might have.

How does a parent answer the question from their child: "Will you come and get me out of jail?"

Some parents will always answer, "Yes." They may find themselves hearing the same question and giving that answer for a lifetime. Some will always answer, "No," believing that "Sarah should learn the hard way." They may also be hearing the same question and giving that an-

---

I Never Thought You'd End Up in Jail!

This phrase may be the most common statement made by parents as their son or daughter is stepping out of the lockup or on the way home from the police station. How frightening and disappointing it is to watch the child whom you can easily remember toddling around the house being processed by the police! Anger, tears, accusations, guilt—all of these are normal reactions.

The above statement is a pretty natural one to make. Take another look at it though. Is that what you really mean? Has your child "ended up?" Is this any more the "end" than any other event in growing up?

Being arrested is usually a one-time event in a child's life. Once is usually enough.

What if it happens? Make it a truly effective experience, so that it will be a one-time experience. Use these suggestions:

1. Treat it as a serious violation of your trust and of the family value system.

2. You will feel hurt: let your hurt show.

3. You will feel fear: let your fear show.

4. You will feel betrayed: require the child to reearn your trust—but make it possible to do so. Remember, this is not the end.

---

swer for a lifetime. It may be well to give this situation some thought ahead of time. The "what, when, how, who, where, and why" questions need to be asked for each situation.

What is the offense? Did it involve a prank gone out of hand? Or was there some deliberate, vicious harm done? Was someone intentionally assaulted or otherwise hurt? Was there a major theft? Exactly what are the facts?

When did the event happen? Did it involve a serious breach of your family curfew?

How was this violation carried out? Did it involve advance planning? Was it childish or adult in nature? How were the culprits apprehended?

Who did what? Is your child really involved? (As in the case in any criminal accusation, call your attorney to find out your options.) Who else was there? Were these people with whom you have discouraged your child's association?

Where did the events happen? Was this someplace that your son or daughter was expected to be? Or was it off limits?

Why may be the hardest question of all. It may also be the most important. It is probably going to be impossible to answer this immediately. But when everyone has calmed down, this needs to be explored thoroughly for the sake of everyone in the family.

Consider the place where the child is being held. Does that holding authority comply with Federal requirements to hold minors in a separate place from adult prisoners? What is the reputation of the police department?

In the last analysis, deciding whether to go and bring your child home from jail immediately, the next day, or in several days is a parental judgment call. Either way, you could be wrong. But, it's one of those situations where you have to make the best choice you can. Although you will be in a very emotional and stressful moment, try to do some analytical introspection and see if the event can be turned toward problem solving. Ask yourself some pointed questions:

What lesson do you want to have learned, and at whose hands?

What has been going on lately in your family life?

How do these events impact your children?

There is no easy answer, but some forethought may help if the question ever arises.

For Family Discussion

Did You Ever?

A minister we know once told the congregation: "One of the things I am most thankful for about my adolescent years is that none of the church members know anything about it!" What did he mean?

Each person might try to think back to a particular time when he did something he knew was wrong. What was it really like?

Why do people break the rules?

Is it adventurous to break the rules?

What are some rewards for breaking the rules?

What was the American attitude toward rules in 1776? What is it now?

Do you have to "draw the line"? Where? How do you decide?

Most young people who commit crimes are experimenters who will not repeat and who will not develop a habit of committing other crimes. It is a mistake, however, to believe that minors cannot be serious criminals. It is hard for middle-class Americans, and especially for suburbanites, to believe that a fourteen-year-old can be dangerous. Yet, it clearly is true. Some, though very few, are as dangerous as any adult. They may even be more so because even habitual adult criminals usually develop some sense of restraint based on their own selfish interests. Adolescents, on the other hand, generally tend to believe they are indestructible. A younger person may not see the deadly consequences of their actions and may act impulsively in ways that do not serve even their own purely selfish interests. It is important for parents to know who their children are spending time with, how they spend their time, who their parents are, and what their rules are.

Meanwhile, be honest and real about your own mistakes. Share with your children what you did that might have brought you into the police station.

"I Only Tried It Once"

Chances are that if you hear that statement, whatever is being described has been tried more than once. Usually this refers to use of a forbidden and harmful substance. How do parents handle drinking and other drug experimentation?

Again, this is a fairly likely occurrence. All of the efforts parents may make to minimize the chance that their child will experiment with alcohol or another drug is not a guarantee. If your home is one in which there is love, support, and expectations leading to a strong self-image, you are reducing the chances for drug use. If you are open in discussing the effects of drugs, you are again reducing the chances. If you and your children can communicate about their feelings, worries, problems, stresses, and temptations, you are further reducing the chances.

But your chances will never be zero.

"Well, We Were on the Couch, and . . ."

When the survival of the species was arranged to happen through sex, the Creator wasn't fooling around. It's meant to happen someday,

Applying the Pledge

1. Be *truthful and honest*

"It was a blast!"

One of the key facts about alcohol and drug use is too seldom recognized and talked about to children: drinking is, in the beginning, exciting, stimulating and fun. The fact that this euphoria is artificial takes a bit longer to grasp.

We seem to be afraid to tell our children this central truth about alcohol and most other drugs: using makes a person feel good. Why else do people get started using? Yet, we very often present to children only the harmful aspects: the hangovers, the effects of addiction, the harm to health, or the death on the highways.

Discussion with children about drugs and alcohol is often purely negative. We may not honestly share with them that these things can taste good. Then, when a child experiments and finds that there is a pretty pleasant result, it may be easy for them to conclude that they were lied to about the rest of it.

Tell the whole truth.

2. Teach and lead *by example.*

"Do as I say and not as I do" is always a silly idea. It is even more so with respect to use of drugs and alcohol.

Use of some alcoholic beverages at meals and other times at family gatherings is often a culturally rooted tradition. Families in some cultures spend many pleasant times when wine or beer is readily in evidence to the children. Yet, many of these families seem to have very little problem with children, or adults, becoming involved in addiction. In every instance, these families are straightforward with children about the dangers of alcohol, while making no attempt to hide its pleasures.

The best use for young people is no use. But the most important determinant is honesty and the setting of the kind of example you want your children to follow.

3. Link performance and outcomes.

Your rule is that your child is not to use alcoholic beverages. Respond positively when they adhere to your high standard; pull back privileges when they don't. Taking corrective action by itself will be ineffective if there is not a good example to follow, but action will make the point that this is something you feel strongly about.

and young, healthy adolescents don't want to wait for it to happen. That doesn't mean they can't wait.

As in the case of alcohol, it is silly to pretend to your adolescent that sex isn't fun and exciting. Their conclusion is perfectly logical: "If there is so much stress on the idea that I must resist doing this, then it must be so good that it's hard to resist!" "Exactly what *is* this thing that I am not supposed to do yet? What is healthy sex, and what is not?

One of the problems unique to our age is the wide presentation of exaggerated, unrealistic sexual fantasies in novels, magazines, movies and television. Children of all ages see and read these fantasies. Parents need to know this and become familiar with them. These media have created unrealistic sexual expectations. Try the honest approach: talk directly and thoroughly about these media materials, sharing them and your thoughts concerning them with your child.

Young people often are worried because they may not feel like doing the things that the novels and media seem to say they should be wanting to do. If they don't feel the unrealistic obsessions depicted, they may think something is wrong with them. Inability to meet these artificial, exaggerated sexual performance expectations can lead to depression in people of all ages.

Work from the base of your personal and family highest faith, vision and values. Why am I in the world? Why have I been endowed with this gift of potential sexual enjoyment? How does this fit in with my values and life plan? Let the children in on the truth: the good, the bad, and the ridiculous. Knowing the facts and building on a strong values system, they will have the best chance of making the right choices.

Show and Tell

It is fundamental logic that if you want to know what something looks like, the best thing is to look. Young children know this. It is a rare child who has not found a way to look over a child of the opposite sex to see what this "boy and girl" business is all about. Often, they will cooperate in this "show and tell" learning experience. When found out, they need to be pretty clearly advised that this is not to happen again, but they don't need to be condemned. It is easy for parents to make too

---

Applying the Pledge

Share love, laughter and life. There is healthy humor in sex, and some of it can be shared with children. There may be the roaming neighborhood tomcat and the resulting, often problematic, kittens appearing at various households. Pubescent boys may experience unexpected, and potentially embarrassing, responses. There can be good humor in all human experiences if accounts are shared responsibly and with imagination.

Sexual expectations are best framed in terms of the overall family value system. How does human sexuality fit into your family's vision and values? There is a good purpose to all things. We do not come into the world equipped with anything intrinsically bad. Our challenge is to learn how to truly use and enjoy all of our strengths. Think through the connection of sexuality to your values, and be prepared to discuss it; "winging it" doesn't work; most kids are too smart for that.

When kids want to talk about sex, asking, listening and hearing is as important as what you may have to say to them. It is more important to know what is on their mind than to tell them what is on your mind. In order to give the right answers, you have to listen to the questions and hear them. If your children know that you are truly interested they will tell you what their questions and worries are. Otherwise, don't be surprised when they act out of ignorance. Giving more information than children are ready to understand, however, can contribute as much to their ignorance as giving too little. You need to know your child thoroughly to assess what they are ready to be told.

Yelling, telling, and commanding is totally futile in this area. Linking performance and outcomes plays a role here. If you make it clear that you expect no "compromising situations" between your adolescent and another, be supportive of their compliance and let them know you are alert to their temptation not to comply. Share your understanding by finding the humor in their situation. "This is a home, not a lover's lane, and watch out for lover's lane, too!"

---

much out of this at an early age. Reasonably supervised play helps the most in keeping this within harmless bounds.

Show, tell, feel, and touch are more typical adolescent temptations. The adolescent who has been told to expect this temptation is not going to be taken by surprise. Again, reasonable parental supervision of boyfriend-girl friend situations will help support adolescents in handling themselves and their feelings. A certain amount of privacy to experience affection can be arranged without "putting the fox in charge of the henhouse." The fox will even appreciate it!

You Can Live Through It!

The problems we have presented here are only a sample of some that parents may experience. We have not dealt in this chapter with depression, unexplained rage, withdrawal, sudden failing grades and many others. Our intent is to present some familiar situations and to outline a general tough-minded approach and to let parents know that they can live through these child-rearing events.

A good general rule is to watch for any sudden changes in the child's actions, attitude, or achievement. It's all right to respect the privacy of children, but their welfare is more important. If you suspect something major is wrong, get into it, find out, and take the needed action. If you need help, get it. But proceed with confidence; you are a parent; you can learn what to do.

You can do it!

12

Live: "Live" Is the Reverse of "Evil"

What does the concept of tough-minded family all boil down to? Can we describe tough-minded family values in a few words? It's simple to talk about—but very tough to consistently discover, internalize, and practice. Here it is:

Love, life, light, and laughter fueled by hope and faith.

Goodness

In trying to define the tough-minded family value system, we are taking on a very difficult, but vitally important task: defining "goodness" in family life. We are defining this "goodness" as being made up of *love, life, light, laughter, hope, and faith.* They are the "parts" of the whole functioning tough-minded family value system.

How can we best understand what these terms really mean in practice? How are they represented in the real world in which you and your children and all of us live? One way to understand anything is to understand its opposite. To truly understand day, we must know the night. To understand light, we need to know what darkness is. What is the opposite of goodness?

Love, life, light, laughter, hope, and faith are real parts of the real world. They are not just abstracts or platitudes that we hear about but never expect to see or experience. They are present and in action in real families around the globe. They are part of the daily experience of our children. Each of these parts or elements is also represented in the real world by an exact opposite. Our children see, hear, and are surrounded by these opposites to goodness as a part of their daily living, just as they are surrounded by the positive values.

187

What is the opposite of a good family values system?

No love, no life, no light, and no laughter fueled by hopelessness and cynicism.

One of the aims of this book is to help parents deal with the real situations that real parents and real children face. We must face reality about life if we are going to be able to deal with it. There are people in the real world actively encouraging lovelessness, or hate; lifelessness, or death; lightlessness, or darkness; corrupted and exploitive laughter, or the taking of pleasure in the inflicting of pain; hopelessness, or the lack of a vision of the future; faithlessness, or cynicism about believing in anything.

Today's world is not unique in having these elements; there have always been plenty of examples of evil to contend with, unique to their time in history. And there are unique manifestations of them today, the modern representations of evil, the counterpoint of goodness.

Scott Peck, a Christian psychiatrist, believes that the greatest threat to the human condition generally, and the family specifically, is a real thing known as evil. In his book, *People of the Lie* (New York: Simon and Schuster, 1983), Peck explores both examples and treatment of this widespread and harmful condition.

In the final section of the book he deals with what he has termed a "Methodology of Love (pp. 265–267)." Some of his key concluding statements are:

> "Specifically, I think we can safely study and treat evil only through the methods of love."
> "Evil can be defeated by goodness."
> "Evil can be conquered only by love."
> "The healing of evil—scientifically or otherwise—can be accomplished only by the love of individuals."

Every family needs a faith with positive beliefs to provide focus to the family value system. The family value system must also deal with the counterpart of goodness, evil. Evil clearly has its attraction. It has great seductive power. It offers short-term rewards that are often hard to resist. Goodness also is attractive. It, too, has great seductive power, although its rewards are often longer term and always more lasting.

C. S. Lewis, Malachi Martin, Erich Fromm, Martin Buber, and others, have written compellingly about what they feel is an omnipresent threat to human beings everywhere.

As C. S. Lewis said in *Christianity and Culture*, contained in *Christian Reflections*, "There is no neutral ground in the universe: Every square inch, every split second is claimed by God and counterclaimed by Satan."

We have pointed out that role models are powerfully important in the formation of a child's value system. It is important to remember that children, and adults as well, become what they hear, think, say, and do. We humans tend to think of ourselves as being what others say we are, and of the world as being what others say it is, especially if those who are saying it are major figures in our lives or in the world.

Evil is a word whose uses has a bad reputation. We see and hear many things in the world around us we know are wrong, harmful, corrupting, or destructive. We are, however, reluctant to openly label these things as being "evil." There is a strong feeling in our society that we should not judge others' actions, that what each person does is "their own business", as long as what they do does not affect me, or innocent people, it's OK.

Tolerance is seen as a virtue. We are not to sit in judgment of others as long as their actions are kept to themselves and they do not affect the rest of the world. We tend, however, to go just beyond this. In practice, our true approach tends to be that what others do is none of my business if it does not affect me or innocent people right this minute. It's OK as long as it does not affect me or my family directly, right now.

Thus, we move from tolerance to complacency. There are practices in the real world that the term "evil" aptly describes, but many of us do not wish to be bothered recognizing this. There are people who actively engage in wrong, harmful, corrupting, or destructive actions. They are advocates of these practices, and may profit from them.

One of the modern manifestations of the actively seductive power of evil is in the lyrics of some—we emphasize *some* but not *all*—"heavy metal" music and "rap" and their methods of presentation. Some of these songs and raps have been best-sellers, avidly heard, viewed, and imitated by millions of children and adolescents from about age eight on up.

The Parent Music Resource Center of Arlington, Virginia, in a video entitled *Rising to the Challenge* presents some of these heavy metal and rap performances. This video asks the question: "The power of colorful television images and attention-getting music to teach children skills, attitudes and behaviors has been amply demonstrated by some of the excellent educational programs; then what is the impact of some of the colorful, attention-getting heavy metal and rap videos?"

Some of these productions and their album covers present violence, rape, masochism, exploitive sex, and Satan worship in very graphic terms. They show attractive role models engaging in and seeming to advocate these practices.

Remember, children, and adults as well, become what they hear, think, say and do.

Making the Home Safe for Children

When infants or young children are going to become a part of the household, or even coming to visit, we scurry around and make sure the house is physically safe for them to be in. Mindful of their instinct to explore, taste, touch, and probe, we remove or secure from their access all sharp objects, pharmaceuticals, soaps, paints, and poisons. Realizing that these are harmful, we see that little children cannot come into contact with them.

Research strongly indicates that explicit lyrics, performances, and cover pictures in some heavy metal videos and recordings have induced children to violence and even suicide. Are these not, then, poison? Your children deserve some privacy about their possessions, but parents are within their duty to make their house as safe for their children as possible by denying permission for these poisonous items to be in the house, anywhere.

Here is where the moral imperative standard applies. You do not have to stand for your morals to be offended by having immoral items in the house. If your position and reasons for this action are firmly but patiently explained, your children will respect your stand.

It might be interesting for you to try to understand and learn to appreciate some of the current popular music; some of it is outstanding; some of it may not be great art, but is still at least decent. It might also be interesting for the family to embark on a study of music together, learning to appreciate the rich variety of music available in our culture.

Consistent with our focus on strengths and gratitude throughout this book is the firm belief that weaknesses can be displaced and replaced by strengths. When we gratefully accept our strengths, we begin the process of accepting ourselves. As we grow to love ourselves, evil cannot invade us.

Scott Peck says, "Is it not evil to love evil?" He consistently makes the point that we only give reality to evil when we think about it and give it attention! Accordingly if we focus consistently, with tough-minded intensity on goodness, evil has no place to take root and grow. Goodness is our wellspring of emotional vigor and health.

Waiting for good things to happen to us, waiting for goodness to come into our lives isn't enough. Parenting is a growth process. We can wisely guide our children if we focus on what is right, what is good, what will work, what goals and dreams can be reached. When our attitude is for-giving and for-loving, we truly lead by our example.

Converting Evil to Good: A Plan of Action

Hans Selye in his classic work, *Stress Without Distress* (New York: Signet Books, 1974) provides us with pragmatic "how-to" for converting evil to good:

> I came to realize that "gratitude" is only one aspect of the broader concept of love, which has been used historically to encompass all positive feelings toward others including respect, goodwill, sympathy and most forms of approval and admiration.
>
> I would consider it the major accomplishment of my life if I could present the case for altruistic egotism so clearly and convincingly as to make it the motto for human ethics in general.
>
> Among all the emotions that—more than any others—account for the presence or absence of harmful stress (distress) in human relations are the feelings of gratitude and goodwill and their negative counterparts, hatred with the urge for revenge.
>
> Finally, never forget that the only treasure that is yours forever is your ability to earn the love of your neighbors.
>
> There will always be leaders and followers, but the leaders are worth

keeping only as long as they can *serve* the followers by acquiring their love, respect, and gratitude.

Evil cannot flourish where love prevails—where real *living* is a reality! Some specific things to begin doing right now are:

1. Set up and begin to build your strength and gratitude notebook. Have vulnerability and gratitude sessions as a family.

2. Be grateful for God, your neighbor, and *you*. As gratitude becomes an attitude, you can hear God when you ask Him to help you fulfill your potential. As you learn to expect much from yourself and actualize these goals, you can begin to expect much from your spouse and your children.

3. Focus on: Love, life, light, laughter.

Love is an all-pervasive healing power. If we decide to choose love instead of hate, we will be loved, and our children will grow in an atmosphere of love. It is that simple. The tough challenge is to consistently make the effort to see goodness where it is easy to see evil; to see potential where it is easy to see weakness; to look for strengths in others when it is easy to point fingers and blame; to focus on what is the truth when it is easier to lie; to be honest and vulnerable when it is easier to be defensive and spiteful. When we feel loved, then we can truly love our children unconditionally.

Life: Our opportunity to *be*. To live in the real and full sense is to reject those practices that qualify as evil. To live is to do the opposite of evil. It may seem naive and simplistic to say it this way, but thinking of *live* as *evil* backwards is accurate. Evil tries to destroy life, but fully living destroys evil.

Light: Choosing a right direction requires light to see the path! We all want to exercise our right to choose our own direction; our own thoughts; our own actions; our own attitudes. When our choices are suffused by faith, love, and integrity; we will become the carriers of the light, showing the way to our children and others who may be struggling against the darkness. "Neither do people light a lamp and put it under a bowl. Instead they put it on its stand and it gives light to everyone in the house" (Matt. 5:15, NIV).

Laughter: The elixir and lubricant for letting go. Reinhold Niebuhr said, "Humor is the prelude to faith and Laughter is the beginning of prayer."

4. Steadily pursue the development of a life in which we are for-"giving" rather than for-"getting".

5. Consistently work at feeling and expressing gratitude to and for God, your children, and *you*. Start counting your blessings and never quit. By creating gratitude and trust, we induce others to share our own natural wish for our own well-being.

You Become What You Say

Some people are aware that we become what we think. Few seem to know, however, that we become what we say. We find in *Expectations and Possibilities* by Joe Batten (New York: Addison-Wesley, 1981, revised 1990):

> When we arrived on planet earth eons ago, it was a verdant place fraught with enormous possibilities. Much that is good, wonderful, and blessed has happened to the human condition. But we have fallen so pitifully short of our possibilities. We have become clothed, swathed, shackled, and stifled—all too often killed—by our attitudes.
> *Our attitudes are at the core of our being.* They condition our biological anatomy, the activation of our brain cells, our choice of nutrition and exercise and, ergo, and condition of our bodies. They condition our relationships with others. *They are truly the agents of change and arbiters of the quality of our lives.*

"As ye sow, so shall ye reap" is one of the greatest statements of truth throughout the history of humankind. We practice this great truth in many ways every day of our lives. The words and behaviors we choose, which are the expressions of our attitudes, pull us into behavior that is good or evil. We do, indeed, become what we say.

We hope that families throughout the world will begin to savor and relish the joy and practicality—the urgency to banish evil—which comes when our vocabularies become charged with words like:

Hope	Lift
Await	Lead
Evoke	Love

Unfold	Create
Expect	Enthusiasm
Share	Give
Dynamic	Eager
Build	Forgive
Faith	Renewal
Empower	Stimulate
Beauty	Delicious
Wonder	Strength
Care	Dream
Vision	Dignity
Gratitude	Freedom
Praise	Grace
Openness	Significance

The ultimate choice is yours. Love or hate—which is your bottom line?

As parents, we have been given the priceless opportunity to help our children become all they can be. There is no greater—or tougher—or more rewarding—privilege! From the moment an infant arrives, the life conditioning begins.

Will they hear you use words that inspire and build, or will they hear words that sow seeds of evil and despair? The choice is yours.

Regardless of circumstances—economic, health, environment, heredity—will you decide to make a relentless effort to provide children with these crucial emotional and mental nutrients? The choice is yours.

Will you choose responsibility, honesty, and integrity—the tough road—or will you back away and opt for an easier and more passive route?

The choice is *yours*.

Above all, remember that if you expect second best, you will get it. If you expect third best, you will get it. If you expect the worst, it will happen. On the other hand, if you consistently expect the best, you will not always get it. But you will achieve much more than any alternative kind of expectation will yield.

Upward on the Path

Emmett Fox, in his book *Power Through Constructive Thinking* gives us some powerful guidelines to move on the upward path to mental health and wholeness:

"I am really on the path:

"If I always look for the best in each person, situation, and thing.

"If I resolutely turn my back on the past, good or bad, and live only in the present and future.

"If I forgive everybody without exception, no matter what he may have done; and if I live to forgive MYSELF wholeheartedly.

"If I regard my job as sacred and do my day's work to the best of my ability (whether I like it or not).

"If I take every means to demonstrate a healthy body and harmonious surroundings for myself.

"If I endeavor to make my life as much service to others as possible, without interfering or fussing.

"If I take every opportunity wisely to spread the knowledge of Truth to others.

"If I rigidly refrain from personal criticism, and neither speak nor listen to gossip.

"If I devote at least a quarter of an hour a day to prayer and meditation.

"If I read at least seven verses of the Bible every day.

"If I specifically claim spiritual understanding for myself every day.

"If I train myself to give the first thought on waking to God.

"If I speak the Word for the whole world every day, say; at dawn.

"If I PRACTICE the Golden Rule of Jesus instead of merely admiring it. He said, 'Whatsoever ye would that men should do to you, do ye even so to them.' The important thing about the Golden Rule is that I am to practice it whether the other fellow does or not."

The choice is yours! Will you *do* it?

Give your children the freedom to fail and be there vulnerably for them when they do. And love them for who they are!

We cannot say too often, we must love ourselves before we can love others. If we expect perfection from our lives and ourselves, we will continually be and feel a failure. No one can be perfect. God gave us the ability to choose and the humanness to learn and grow. We grow by stretching ourselves to be a little bit better than we may think we can; by setting realistic challenges rather than impossible goals of perfection.

Share your failures with your children along with your goals, your dreams. Let your children feel the freedom to share their fears and failure, hopes, and dreams, with you. You can only help them succeed if you understand what they want to be.

Life!

Tough-minded parenting is a journey through life. The principles we have presented are rooted in the wisdom of successful parents from the present, the recent past, and the great stretch of human history. You and your children are the link with the future, the tough-minded parents of tomorrow.

Life is the unfailing antidote to death. Life is your gift to your children and theirs to you.

To live is to grow. Enjoy your life with them—grow with them—and watch them grow.

Glossary of Terms

Abuse Deliberate misuse of a person who is under your power with intent to harm.

  Emotional abuse Use of words, tones of voice, or actions that cause emotional pain.

  Physical abuse Deliberate physical harm to another person.

  Sexual abuse Using a person sexually.

Accountability The "ability to account" for the extent to which a commitment is met or for any action or inaction for which the family member is responsible.

Action Plan A sequenced and prioritized chronology of intent, commitment, and tactics: what one is going to get done and some of the key activities involved.

Activity Motion toward a clearly targeted result, something one *does*, as contrasted with something one gets *done* (result).

Addiction The process of compulsive, habitual use of drugs resulting in withdrawal when the drug is stopped; often characterized by tolerance.

Advise To give information to; to externally impose; not to be confused with counsel which asks, listens, and develops a consensus of follow-up.

Aggressiveness Initiative that is primarily self-serving. Not to be confused with assertiveness, which uses one's strengths for purpose of building.

Alcoholism A chronic, fatal, progressive disease, which is characterized by an inability to control drinking.

Appraisal To determine the value and possibilities that are implicit in a person's performance and personality at a particular time.

197

Ask To request a response from another; to seek the response and reaction of another. Asking another affirms their dignity and worth.

Assertiveness The vulnerable exposure of strengths. Since strengths are all we possess, and thus all we have to assert, vulnerability permits the full use of these strengths without defensiveness.

Autonomy Self-directed freedom based on moral independence.

Builder The parent who stands tall is, above all, a builder. Committed to vision, stretch, empowerment, synergy, responsiveness, and flexibility—toughness of mind—a builder ensures that all dimensions are intensely focused on creation, growth, and building.

Candor Applied truth. In the tough-minded lexicon, this involves openness, vulnerability, awareness of the needs of others, and a genuine desire to build them.

Caring Consistent manifestation of concern for and affirmation of others. The perception that all people are right until proven wrong and that each person is a bundle of strengths and possibilities.

Climate The temperature of the human environment in which one finds oneself; the "feel," the "chemistry," often more sensed than known.

Climate for Mistakes An environment that calls for and reinforces constant experimentation, creativity, innovation, and change. Encourages the practice of "failing forward." Mistakes within reason are *rewarded* rather than penalized.

Co-dependence The effect of the addiction of a family member on the family as a whole such that all adjust their lives to that addiction and become dependent on it.

Command To order or demand with authority. Justified only in emergency situations.

Commitment An internalized, then externalized, concentration of desire and energy focused on various degrees of achievement. An "integrity of intent."

Communication Shared meaning, shared understanding, attained by asking, listening, and hearing.

Compensation Providing or receiving full value, psychological or financial, for energy expended.

Conditional Love To extend love accompanied by extenuations, provisos, and retained conditions and defined circumstances.

Confront To address openly, honestly, and vulnerably that which needs to be addressed. The reverse of expedience, obliqueness, deviousness, or avoidance.

Consistency Consonance of thought, word or deed over a continuum of time, space, or relationships.

Consultive Decision Making A decision-making process in which the parent involves family members and secures their best input prior to making any major decisions.

Control—Parental An end result of interactive processes involving clarity of expectation and the achievement thereof. Control is not a tool per se. It is a *result* of excellence in applying the other concepts in the tough-minded parenting system.

Coordinate Shared meaning and shared understanding that permit and require the synchronized effort of appropriate people to achieve mutually understood goals.

Counsel To help others develop insights and actions to achieve mutually understood goals. This pertains particularly to helping one identify, surface, fuse, and focus one's present and potential strengths to lead and guide toward goal achievement.

Criticize To evaluate the results of analyses and identify the values or strengths therein. To build on those strengths in seeking to improve the situation, person, or thing.

Develop To generate, synthesize, nurture, and ultimately create something better.

Denial Pretending to yourself and/or others that something you would rather not face is not real.

Dignity The worth, significance, and uniqueness of a person; one's awareness of intrinsic worth. Clear, consistent expectations and a constant search for and focus on strengths develop and affirm dignity.

Directive Words or actions, felt or implied, that arbitrarily state an action or result desired. A command. Tend to suggest "compression and pushing" rather than "evolking and stretching" (as in expective). Useful only in emergency situations.

Discipline Training and development that builds, molds, and strengthens lean, clean, focused behavior. Adherence to discipleship of a positive value system.

Dissatisfaction A preoccupation with *past* failures; a tendency to dwell on what didn't work. On the contrary *un*satisfaction is a healthy, hungry desire to change, grow, and move onward and upward.

Dream A deeply felt hope of the possible. Dreams lift and move individuals and organizations to the highest levels of performance.

Dysfunction Function that is flawed or inadequate; where difficulties exist that are not readily solved.

Dysfunctional Family A family which is not functioning well.

Emotional Stimulus Elicitation of emotions needed to ensure that knowledge or information is transmuted and transmitted into learning. A gestalt of feelings.

Empower To create and foster a relationship in which all of the persons understand their significance, possibilities, and strengths. People who are empowered have a clear understanding of their authority, responsibility, accountability, and valued family role and they have autonomy that is symbiotic with others.

Empathy The imaginative projection of one's consciousness into the consciousness of another. The ability to put yourself in the other person's shoes.

Enabler One who inadvertently helps the dependent (addict?) to continue drinking or using; one who helps make possible the continuing of any undesirable habitual behavior.

Evaluate To identify the relative value of an action, a person, place, or thing, or relationship; the values (strengths) implicit in a person's performance and personality at a particular time.

Evil The opposite of life and goodness.

Excellence What happens when you give an undertaking your best shot—and know it.

Expectation A desire, want, or need communicated in the form of a clear request. The ultimate gift, it says to others, "I value and appreciate your possibilities."

Faith Belief in and trust and loyalty to God. Belief in and commitment to causes, quests, and affirmations that transcend self-concern. Complete confidence in something without requirement of proof.

Family Parents and their children; descendants of one common ancestor; people so related who live together in mutually supportive relationships.

Family Mission Statement A statement of the beliefs and goals guiding your family. Usually created by the family working together.

Fake One who is affected, self-deprecating, insincere, overly subtle, hence, evasive and untrustworthy. One who retreats from the requirements of self-discipline.

Feedback Information that clearly indicates the progress and corrective needs of the ongoing project or undertaking. The giving of indications that communication is understood.

Flexibility and Resilience The opposite of *rigidity*. The living and committed responsiveness to possibilities, difficulties, and opportunities.

Forgive To extend understanding, clemency, and pardon; to relinquish feelings of hurt and resentment.

G-Forces The figurative pull of gravity. Negative G forces of the past are passive, self-defeating attitudes and practices that retard and even reverse forward movement. Positive "G" forces of the future are passionate attitudes and practices that help pull and guide the person to move toward the future in a most productive, energetic, and positive way.

Give Sharing one's self and/or belongings. Directing one's major energies toward providing encouragement, knowledge, inspiration, and understanding rather than seeking self-aggrandizement.

Goal Something one wishes to accomplish. Broader and more timeless than an objective. Expressed as a desired and targeted happening. Drawn from a system of values.

Go-giver A positive term replacing the cliché "go-getter"; a tough-minded person who knows that one can achieve much more when major energies are directed toward giving encouragement, knowledge, inspiration, and understanding to others rather than seeking self-aggrandizement only.

Grace A special warmth felt and expressed toward all other human beings; an absence of pettiness and self-concern. A living manifestation of the belief that a person should devote major energies to doing something *for* others and not *to* others. Flows from a focused faith.

Gratitude Thoughts, feelings, and actions that reflect and transmit appreciation and earned praise.

Hard Rigid, compressed, repressed, depressed, oppressed, dead, weak. The *reverse* of toughness.

Hear To go beyond mere listening; to understand and comprehend; shared meaning; shared understanding.

Heart The core of one's being; one's inmost feelings.

Honesty Free from deceit; free from fraud and obfuscation; integrity in expression and action. Truth. Candor.

Hope To desire with belief in possibility of attaining; a feeling replete with ingredients of love, faith, significance, and gratitude.

Individual One whole, identifiable and distinct person. Distinguished from "rebel." Rebels live, talk, and work in terms of what they are *against*; individuals live, talk, and work in terms of what they are for.

Integrity Strength, reality, authenticity, toughness, realness.

Intuition The capacity to take correct actions without necessarily knowing why. A feel, a sense, a sensation in the gut of what is appropriate. Quick and ready insight.

Involvement Joint and shared use of talents to develop, clarify, and achieve results.

Judge To form subjective conclusions about another person. Distinct from *evaluate*.

Kinesics "Body English." The study of body movements, facial expressions, and so on as ways of communicating.

Lead To be in front, figuratively. To lift, guide, expect, demonstrate, empower, communicate, and achieve results.

Leadership The exercise of a system of expectations designed to mobilize and maximize the most effective use of strengths to achieve growth.

Listen To attend closely to; to yield to advice; to perceive the words used by another; to be cognizant of others' attempts to communicate.

Love A very deep feeling of goodwill toward others. Tough-minded parents express love with a disciplined commitment to build rather than destroy, to enhance rather than to diminish all family members through every thought, word, and action.

Loving Trust Conveying the best expectations through being informed and involved. Loving trust takes into account the readiness of the child to receive a given trust, as well as the other adults, peers, and circumstances in the situation.

Loyalty A quality or action of steadfastly adhering to one's beliefs in a person or thing by every thought, word, or action. See Faith.

Mentor An experienced, wise, and prudent counselor; one who leads the mentee toward positive solutions and planned actions.

Mission A stretching, guiding, and reinforcing statement of intent and commitment.

Motivation Motive-action; "action to achieve motive."

Motive The reason one wishes to see something done.

Negative stress Stress which causes destruction of or inhibits strength, vitality or ability to act effectively.

Nurture To care for. To provide insights, expectations, reinforcement, asking, listening, and hearing that stimulate people to grow.

Objective Something one wants to *get done*. A specific statement of quality, quantity, and time values.

Open Listening Truly open hearing with heart, mind, and soul. A felt and expressed desire to truly understand the other person, like "Empathy."

Organize To blend resources logistically to achieve objectives; to deploy strengths logically.

Passion Intense, focused feelings fed by the value system described in this book.

Passive Yielding, quiescent, nonresponsive, with a low level of reaction. The opposite of active.

Plan An orderly assortment of actions designed to fulfill a mission or accomplish a goal or objective. An objective by itself is not a plan; it is only the basis for one.

Positive Stress Exertion that results in strengthening and growth. Healthy, focused energy applied to positive goals.

Power Capacity to do something. Qualities emanating from the parent that exert direction and attraction, purpose and pull. Positive, forward-focused influence.

Purpose An overriding, lifting, stretching end to be attained.

Quality The degree of excellence a thing possesses. Also see total quality.

Renewal Innovation and renovation. The process of making fresh, strong, and good; new physical, mental, and spiritual strength.

Respect Feelings, felt and expressed, that reflect enhanced awareness of the dignity, worth, and individuality of another person.

Responsibility Response ability, or ability to respond. Responding in a manner consistent with full integrity.

Results The final happening as a consequence of action. Not to be confused with a measurement of a result.

Self-confidence A growing awareness of your own strengths and, often, a heightened zest for strong, testing, and confrontive challenges.

Self-discipline Commitment of "self-in-discipleship" to worthwhile courses of action. Most effective when focused on goals that transcend personal gain.

Self-esteem The belief that you are significant and good.

Service The ongoing product of a passionate commitment to fulfill the wants, needs, and possibilities of others.

Significance The feeling that a person "counts," is real and is accomplishing good, stretching, and relevant things in life.

Strengths The true realities in all persons and things. Conversely, weaknesses are only what is absent or lacking. Strengths are the only building blocks to anything, the only resources one can employ in every dimension of life.

Strengths notebook A personal listing containing an individual's salient strengths.

Stress See positive stress.

Stretch A questing, reaching, searching for a better way.

Symbiosis A relationship where living or working together provides and enhances mutual advantage.

Synergy The magnified impact of a confluence or synthesis of strengths. In shorthand, $2 + 2 = 5$ or more. The whole is greater than the sum of the parts.

System of Values A complete and functionally compatible combination of essential truths. Values are the subjective interpretation of the immutable laws of the universe that shape and guide human reactions. The orderly expression and transfer of tough-minded values into practices is the essential process involved in building a unified family.

Tell To order or command; to demand acquiescence; to impose one's desires on another person; often has a diminishing effect on the recipient.

Tomorrow-Mindedness Living to anticipate, create, and innovate the future. A tomorrow-minded parent is responsive rather than reactive.

Tool A usable resource or combination of resources to instrument a desired level of achievement. Something one usually employs directly to get something done. May be a personal skill or understanding.

Tough The integrity of a substance, person, place, thing, or feeling. Characterized by tenacity, resilience, flexibility, durability, and suppleness.

Tough-minded Open, resilient, growing, changing, questing, stretching quality of mind. Having an infinite capacity for growth and change.

Tough-minded Parent The parent, who, much like a compass, provides love, example, direction, leadership, and pull. The TMP "walks in front of the flock" and exemplifies the system of values and practices this book is all about.

Trust The feeling that expectations will be met. The implicit belief in the integrity, or strength of the potential behavior of another person. The knowledge that there will be realness and honesty.

Unconditional Love Love with no strings attached to extend full understanding, full commitment and belief in the essential goodness and rightness of another person. The opposite of conditional love.

Unity Oneness of purpose, focus, communication, and action.

Unsatisfaction A healthy and hungry desire for new growth, new effectiveness, new levels of achievement. Distinct from dissatisfaction.

Value The intrinsic worth (or strength) of any action or thing. See "System of Values."

Vision A transcendent view of the possible.

Vital Bursting with life and positively directed energy.

Vulnerable Openness to experiences. Affirmation of belief in the essential goodness and rightness of life. The absence of defensive, petty, or suspicious behavior.

Warmth Emotion and caring, flowing toward others, that transmits feelings of affirmation, reassurance, and love. Overt evidence of a desire to build and give to another, reflected in tone of voice, facial expression, and the free expression of positive emotion.

Wisdom The ability or gift of transcendent vision. To see the "big picture," to visualize the immediate need or problem in proper perspective. A knowledge of fundamental truths and the ability to use them in a meaningful developmental and positive way.

Appendix A: Personal & Family Mission Statements

Stephen R. Covey

"Our peculiar security is in the possession of a written Constitution" (Thomas Jefferson).

Mission statements, whether personal, family, or corporate in scope, empower people to unify, focus, and take control of their lives. In writing a mission statement, you are drawing a blueprint, raising a standard, drafting a constitution.

The project deserves broad involvement. In my experience, every family or company that has conscientiously involved its members in formulating a mission statement has produced a fine constitution. The principle is basic to our society: govern (manage) by the consent of the people.

We have in America a glorious constitution. John Adams said that the Constitution of the United States was written for a moral people. The U.S. Constitution is fundamentally changeless. In over two hundred years, we've had only twenty-six amendments, ten of which were in the original Bill of Rights. It's the standard for evaluating all laws; the document the president agrees to defend and support; the criteria for admitting people into citizenship.

Personal Mission Statement

Your personal constitution should reflect what you value most. It should serve as a basis for making major, life-directing decisions, providing you with a sense of personal identity and internal security, a changeless core, a constant sense of who you are, what you are about, and what you value.

When your security comes from within, you can adapt to changes

from without. You can afford to be open, to drop prejudices and stereotypes, and to stop categorizing everything and everybody. You can handle diversity and complexity. You become more proactive. You have the
values for directing your life, for setting short- and long-term goals. You
have a constitution for measuring every decision concerning the best
use of your time, talents, and energies.

Whatever is at the center of a person's life serves as a lens through
which life is viewed. People who center on work, spouse, family, friends,
enemies, possessions, money, pleasure, or church have a tough time
maintaining balance. Meanwhile, people who center on a set of proven
principles enjoy three important benefits:
   • *security* not to be threatened by change, comparisons or criticisms;
   • *guidance* to make wise decisions;
   • *power* to communicate and cooperate effectively, even under conditions of stress and fatigue.

A personal and family mission statement can help keep us centered
on what really matters most. Our security comes from knowing that
principles, unlike people or things, do not change—we can depend on
them. Our wisdom and guidance come from correct maps that help us
to see clearly where we want to go and how to get there. And our
power comes from principle-centered living, enabling us to balance
our energy and talent in free-flowing, proactive ways. Thus anchored,
we have no need to build our emotional lives on the weaknesses of
others.

Family Mission Statements

Many families are managed on the basis of crises, moods, quick fixes,
and instant gratification, not on sound principles. Symptoms surface
whenever stress and pressure mount: people start yelling, overreacting,
or being cynical, critical, or silent. Children see this and think it's the
way you solve problems—fight or flight. And the cycle can be passed
on for generations.

In writing a family mission statement, you work on the foundation.
The core of any family is what is changeless, what is always going to be
there—and this is what is represented in a family constitution. We
recently reviewed our family's mission. We involved every family mem-

ber, came up with several key purpose and value statements, and then condensed these into one sentence:

The mission of our family is to create a nurturing place of order, truth, love, happiness, and relaxation and to provide opportunities for each person to become responsibly independent and effectively interdependent in order to serve worthy purposes in society.

Just as our national constitution is the supreme law of the land and the basis for evaluating everything else, a family mission statement becomes a constitution to the degree it is used daily to direct and evaluate all family plans and activities.

Writing Your Constitution

I agree with the wise philosopher who said that we direct rather than invent our missions in life. I think each of us has an internal monitor or conscience that gives us an awareness of our own uniqueness and the singular contributions that we can make. Focusing on what we want to be and do is the first step in creating a mission statement.

Of course, a mission statement is not something you write overnight. It takes careful introspection, careful analysis, and thoughtful expression to produce it in final form. The process may take several weeks, even months, before you feel comfortable with it. Even then, you may want to make minor changes as the years bring new insights and circumstances.

Remember: the process is just as important as the product. Writing a mission statement changes you because you are forced to think through your priorities carefully and then to align your behavior with your beliefs. As you do, other people begin to sense that you're not being driven by everything that happens to you. You have a sense of mission about what you're trying to do, and you're excited about it.

To help give expression to those things deep within you, I suggest you take the following steps:

First, expand your perspective. We become so involved with the day-to-day activities of life that it's usually necessary to stand back to gain or expand perspective and remind ourselves what really matters.

I recently reviewed my own mission statement, which I do on an annual basis. Sitting alone on a beach, I began thinking about my life and started taking some notes. After a while, I began to feel a sense of clarity, a sense of organization and commitment, a sense of exhilaration and freedom. I've found that once "on paper" and "in heart," a mission statement is liberating and empowering.

These "perspective experiences" may be planned or unplanned. Unplanned experiences may include the death and funeral of a loved one, a severe illness, a financial setback, or extreme adversity. At such times, we stand back, look at our lives, and ask ourselves some hard questions: What do we consider most important? Why are we doing what we're doing? If we didn't have to do what we do to get money, what would we do? Through this self-evaluation process, we tend to expand our perspective.

Use the tremendous visualizing power of your right brain to expand perspective. Don't tie yourself to your past, rather tap into your potential. Live out of your imagination, not out of your memory. The best way to predict your future is to create it. Write your own eulogy. Visualize your fiftieth wedding anniversary or your retirement. What contributions, what achievements will you want to have made? What plans? Visualize them in detail. Think in terms larger than today and next year.

Think of your life in terms of roles and goals. Consider the various roles of your life. Think of your family roles, professional roles, church roles, or community roles. You probably play a number of different roles, and each is important. Defining your roles and goals will help give you balance. Keep these roles in front of you and review them frequently to make sure that you don't get totally absorbed by one role to the exclusion of others that are equally or even more important in your life. Otherwise, you may climb a certain ladder of success only to discover later that it's leaning against the wrong wall.

Next, consider the goals you hope to accomplish in each of your chosen roles. Make them your goals, reflecting your deepest values and your unique talents.

Draft a statement and get feedback on it. After expanding perspective, defining roles, and considering goals, charge someone with the responsibility of drafting the mission statement, taking into account what has been gathered and shared so far.

Invite feedback. Revise it. Use some wording from different family members. A statement that is well worded gives tremendous focus to the family. One that is not well refined will not be as valuable and useful in decision making. The best mission statements are the result of people coming together in a spirit of mutual respect, expressing their different views, and working together to create something greater than any one individual could do alone.

An Ongoing Process

The very process of writing and refining a mission statement becomes a key way to improve the family. Do it periodically to expand perspective, shift emphasis or direction, amend or give new meaning to time-worn phrases.

The mission statement becomes a framework for thinking, for governing. Review it frequently and ask, "Are we doing the best we can to live by this? Are we preventing problems?" Management by quick fix leads to management by crises. Crises come one after another just like a pounding surf. Troubles come so frequently that life begins to blend into one huge problem. Cynicism and fatigue set in.

By having a constitution, you have continuity. This is one of the major benefits of managing and leading by a mission statement developed through a participative process. And, when individual values are harmonized with those of the family, members work together for common purposes that are deeply felt.

And the bottom line is that things don't just get a little better, they get dramatically better.

Dr. Stephen R. Covey is the Founder and Chief Executive Officer of the Covey Leadership Center, Provo, Utah.

Appendix B: Family Finance

R. Patrick McGoldrick

Parents spend little time training their children in the area of finances. A young person today grows up often receiving an allowance, but with no financial guidance as to how to save or spend those first dollars.

Children are presented with the opportunity to become spenders very early in life—and the chance to get hooked on credit. They are stimulated from infancy to want material things: the best toys, designer-label clothing, and all the rest. No sooner do they graduate from high school than they receive offers for credit cards from all the various vendors and banks. Companies particularly promote cards for college students in the belief that they will either be able to pay their bills or their parents will pay for them.

They then enter life, and maybe form a family, with no knowledge of the tools available for financial success and frequently carrying debt from college, car loans, credit cards, and poor money management.

It is obvious that as a part of everyone's training in life, time should be spent in the home or schools teaching basic financial discipline, the importance of savings, the importance of spending within one's means, and the importance of using credit wisely.

The concerns of children today are frequently the result of a dysfunctional, neglectful environment. Parental neglect is often reflected in poor financial planning along with its other manifestations. Many parents just don't know the basics.

What are the basics?

1. Save for yourself first.
2. Live within your budget, and budget realistically.

212

3. Establish a monthly plan and a yearly plan, including what you project to earn and what you project to spend.

4. Avoid impulse buying.

5. Use caution when applying credit to your purchases.

Budgeting is the place to begin. A good, sound financial budget for young people would include a percentage for savings. If young people would save 15 percent of whatever they receive, many of their financial worries of the future would be solved.

A special note on credit: Throughout life, regardless of how poor your financial condition might be, someone will always give you credit. The real question is what is the price for that credit? We often see young people who have debt well over their income, 25 or 30 percent of which is going toward the maintenance of that debt. In other words, it is going toward the interest payments to keep the debt from going any higher. It is very hard to get ahead financially in that kind of scenario.

Finally, if you are confused and don't understand basics, either go to the library and read books on finances or call a financial planner and ask for some help in developing a basic plan for your future.

R. Patrick McGoldrick, CLU is president of McGoldrick-Blau Financial Planners, Inc. of Des Moines, Iowa.

Appendix C: Suggested Reading List for Parents

Albert, Linda and Popkin, Michael. *Quality Parenting*. NY: Random House, 1987.

Batten, Joe D. *Expectations and Possibilities*. Santa Monica, CA: Hay House, 1990.

Batten, Joe D. *Tough-Minded Leadership*. NY: AMACOM, 1989.

Berends, Polly Berrien. *Whole Child/Whole Parent*. NY: Harper & Row, 1983.

Bettelheim, Bruno. *A Good Enough Parent*. NY: Alfred A. Knopf, 1987.

Cutright, Melitta J. *The National PTA Talks to Mothers*. New York: Doubleday, 1989.

Dobson, James. *Dare to Discipline*. Wheaton, IL: Tyndale House Publishers, 1981.

Dobson, James. *Hide or Seek*. Old Tappan, NJ: Fleming H. Revell, 1979.

Dobson, James. *The Strong-Willed Child*. Wheaton, IL: Tyndale House Publishing, 1978.

Dyer, Wayne W. *What Do You Really Want for Your Children?* NY: William Morrow & Company, Inc., 1985.

Ehrensoft, Diane. *Parenting Together*. NY: Free Press, 1987.

Fettig, Art. "The Three Robots" series. Battle Creek, Michigan: Growth Unlimited, Inc., 1981.

Ford, Edward E. and Englund, Steven. *For the Love of Children*. NY: Anchor Press/ Doubleday, 1977.

Kiley, Dan. *Nobody Said It Would Be Easy*. NY: Harper & Row, 1978.

Kokin, Morris and Walker, Ian. *Women Married to Alcoholics*. NY: William Morrow & Company, 1989.

Milgram, Gail Gleason, Ed. D. *What, When, and How to Talk to Children About Alcohol and Other Drugs.* Center City, MN: Hazelden, 1983.

Newman, Susan. *You Can Say No to a Drink Or a Drug.* NY: Perigee Books, 1986.

Oberender, Kay Hill and Pearce, William N. *Scruffy Shares a Secret.* Des Moines, IA: Powell III Publications, 1989.

Packard, Vance. *Our Endangered Children.* Boston: Little, Brown and Company, 1983.

Rosenberg, Ellen. *Growing Up Feeling Good.* NY: Beaufort Books, 1987.

Schiamberg, Lawrence B. and Smith, Kael V. *Human Development.* NY: Macmillan, 1982.

Appendix D: Food and Family Life: A Brief on Nutrition

Donald Baldwin, D.C.
Gwendy Peters, D.C.

Contrary to popular belief, based on the appearance of abundance, malnutrition is very real in America and other Western cultures. While the medical community sees few cases of scurvy or beriberi, what we are discussing here is more analogous to a slow, chronic, cumulative, and deliberately self-inflicted poisoning.

One may point to the "enriched bread," "fortified milk," and other improved products and say "Look at all the vitamins and minerals added to what we eat." But, what do we eat, really?

If any of us wrote in a daily diary every bite and drink, then calculated the nutritional value or destructive effects, we might be horrified to find that we are actually starving ourselves. We would find that we are in a rather constant state of craving, which is the body's way of begging for "something." Without a good understanding of nutrition, our instant-gratification society teaches us to reach for the first and fastest food available. This is instant gratification of a perceived need rather than of the real need.

And instant gratification is our heritage. Though we see it happening continually, it should still be obvious that food is not to be used for gaining the desired behavior of a child, as potato chips, cookies, candy, beverages, etc., frequently are. "Be good and you can have some . . ."

For many of our children, breakfast is the latest commercial fad, sugar-coated cereal from TV, or a premade pastry, and a can of soda.

Breakfast means literally "to break the fast." The "fast being the period of time from the last meal of the previous day until the first meal of the morning. The blood sugar, which is derived from food to fuel the body, has dropped to a low point. The body must maintain a certain

216

balance in blood sugar. Sudden infusion of sugar may result in a high level followed quickly by a new low. This results in the "midmorning slump" that the candy and soda commercials tell us requires the boost from their product. This leads to a blood sugar roller-coaster effect of highs and lows.

Some of the more obvious effects of low blood sugar include feeling sluggish and depressed, slow mental activity, anxiety, belligerence, nausea, hunger, headache, and muscular shakes. Does this sound familiar? What is actually needed for breakfast, as for any meal, is a balance of protein, fats, and complex carbohydrates that will break down at a pace that will maintain adequate blood sugar throughout the day.

There was a time when school lunch was a meal designed by dietitians and supervised by an adult to see that children ate it. Now, with the advent of junk-food choices offered at school, unless the child has learned at home to make wise decisions about eating habits, the likelihood of a student eating a right balance is almost nonexistent.

How many of our teenagers are drinking high-caffeine beverages to stay awake in the afternoon because their blood sugar drops too fast? Junk foods quickly turn to sugar or fat. Some of the young bodies in our schools may look healthy, but many are not. Add to the stress of improper diet those of athletics, brain work, a job, social worries, and all the normal pressures of life for a young person and you have a tremendous drain on the body. They cannot possibly function to the optimum.

Might nutrition have an impact on the relative rarity of the bright-eyed, fresh-faced, eager-to-learn look in classrooms?

Myths

1. "Good nutrition costs more than bad nutrition." In fact, the reverse is true. What is required is more time to plan, select, purchase, and prepare foods wisely. A general rule of thumb: The more preparation and processing by the manufacturer before you buy, the less nutritive value that is likely left in the product. Ideally, straight from garden to mouth, or the closest thing to it you can devise. Read the labels!

2. "Nutritious food doesn't taste good and the kids won't eat it." Most patients tell us that after only a short time on a low-salt or low-sugar diet if they happen to eat some of the their former "regular" food, their

mouth burned or they felt ill. They were now able to truly taste food for the first time.

There are many good sources in the library for information about good eating. Here are some quotes from one example, *The American Medical Guide* (New York: Random House 1982) p. 26.

1. Eat meat no more than once a day. Fish and poultry are less fattening than red meat, sausages, and processed meats.

2. Bake or broil meat rather than frying it. If you do fry, use polyunsaturated oils such as corn oil rather than butter, lard or saturated margarines.

3. Cut down on salt and other sodium containing substances such as monosodium glutamate (MSG). Do not salt your food without tasting it first.

4. Get your daily quota for fiber by eating plenty of vegetables and fruit. Eat them raw or lightly cooked, because prolonged cooking destroys the vitamins. Another good source of fiber is potato skins. A food does not have to have a tough or stringy texture to contain fiber.

5. Do not eat more than a total of four eggs a week. Although they are low in saturated fats, eggs have a very high cholesterol content.

6. For dessert or a snack, choose fresh fruit (without cream) rather than cookies, cakes, or puddings.

Finally, remember that the saying, "Everything in moderation" has a great deal of merit. Too much of anything, whether it be the number of calories you consume or a certain kind of food, is unwise. A balanced diet taken in moderation along with adequate exercise cannot guarantee good health, but is a big help in maintaining health.

Donald L. Baldwin and Gwendy R. Peters/Baldwin are doctors of chiropractic medicine and consultants in nutrition in Iowa.

Appendix E: Self-Discovery Worksheets

As a person and a parent, who am I? Where am I going? How do I move in that direction? Who are we as a family, and where are we going? What can we do together to move in the way we want to go?

Here are some exercises you might use to help you with these basic questions. As a parent, look them over and think about them. Get the family together and work on them, maybe over a period of time.

It can be interesting to complete them, then do them again in a year, or half a year, and compare to see what has changed or what progress has been made.

After the family has utilized these tools, they might try to invent new listings or exercises that are even more effective for their needs.
Good luck!

Self-discovery Work Sheets

I. *My Strengths*

I am defined and profiled by my strengths. My weaknesses only tell me what additional strengths I need. I will pursue greater knowledge of my strengths for the rest of my life. I believe this and am going to take the following steps to ensure that this practice becomes a living part of me:

Five situations or problems I have met as a parent before I utilized my strengths and potential

	Problem	New strengths	How I can use them
1.			
2.			
3.			
4.			
5.			

II. *Strengths of My Family*

When I focus inwardly in a quest for self, all is ultimately lost. When I reach out and focus on the possibilities all around me, I discover who, what and why I am. I believe this and I am going to take the following steps to ensure that this knowledge becomes a living part of me:

Five situations where I must focus my children's and spouse's strengths:

	Situation	Strengths	How they can be used
1.			
2.			
3.			

4.

5.

III. *Example*

   Integrity is what I AM, what I BELIEVE, what I FEEL, and what I
DO. Sound ethics are always renewing in the long run. The problem is
one of living up to these beliefs. What I AM can thunder so loud they'll
WANT to hear what I SAY. I believe this and am going to take the
following steps to establish and use a system of attitudes and values that
excite me and that I can use and live each day:

These are my values and beliefs	*This is how I can use them*	*This is my example to my children*
1.		
2.		
3.		
4.		
5.		
6.		
7.		
8.		
9.		
10.		

IV. *Confidence*

The most scarce ingredient in business and daily living today is deep, sustaining self-confidence. To do only the expedient means I need more confidence in my decisions. Self-confidence provides the building blocks for the temple that is me. This is the person I hope to become.

What I need to change to like myself more	*Values and strengths needed*	*Strengths I have already*
1.		
2.		
3.		
4.		
5.		
6.		

V. *Hidden Beauty*

I will build into every action, every thought, and every reaction the belief that negativism is NEVER justified. It is one of the great mistakes of our current way of life that we assume that "criticism" means pointing out weaknesses. It really means a SEARCH for HIDDEN BEAUTY. To evaluate another person is to seek to know and identify their values and strengths. I will search for that spark of the divine that dwells in every person.

I believe this and am going to take the following steps:

          For myself   *For my children*

1.

2.

3.

4.

5.

VI. *The New Parent*

This is the parent I hope to become:

Values and strengths needed   *Strengths I am already using*